J. WESTON
WALCH
PUBLISHER
Portland, Maine

Content-Area Reading Strategies

Language Arts

Ben Brenneman

User's Guide
to
Walch Reproducible Books

Purchasers of this book are granted the right to reproduce all pages.

This permission is limited to a single teacher, for classroom use only.

Any questions regarding this policy or requests to purchase further reproduction rights should be addressed to

Permissions Editor
J. Weston Walch, Publisher
321 Valley Street • P.O. Box 658
Portland, Maine 04104-0658

1   2   3   4   5   6   7   8   9   10
ISBN 0-8251-4572-4

Copyright © 2003
J. Weston Walch, Publisher
P.O. Box 658 • Portland, Maine 04104-0658
walch.com

Printed in the United States of America

Contents

INTRODUCTION
To the Teacher

Content-Area Reading Strategies teaches students how to read to learn. In the early grades, students learn to read and write narratives—stories. They are used to dealing with texts that have a beginning, a middle, and an end. They expect to encounter rising action that leads to a climax and then to a resolution.

This pattern of organization is often not followed in informational texts, which begin to make up a large portion of classroom-related reading about grade four. Without instruction in how to read these kinds of nonnarrative texts, even "good" readers can stumble. Some research shows that the so-called "fourth-grade reading slump" may be attributable in part to the unsupported transition from narrative to informational texts.

That's where the *Content-Area Reading Strategies* series comes in. Each book in the series focuses on a different content area and gives students concrete tools to read informational texts efficiently, to comprehend what they read, and to retain the information they have learned.

Organization is an important part of comprehending and retaining knowledge. The graphic organizers in *Content-Area Reading Strategies* help students connect new information to their existing schemata, increasing their ability to recall and take ownership of what they read. The reading strategies give students a way to "see" what they read—a great asset to visual learners.

The reading-writing connection is a strong one. The reading strategies in this book all require students to record information in writing, strengthening readers' ability to retain and access newly acquired knowledge.

Classroom Management

Content-Area Reading Strategies is easy to use. Simply photocopy each lesson and distribute it. Each lesson focuses on a single strategy and includes models showing the strategy in action. At the back of this book, there is a blank copy of each graphic organizer, so you can copy them as often as needed. Quiz questions assess how well students understood what they read.

The Practice Readings provide longer readings and questions. For these, you may want to let students choose which strategy to use, or you may assign a particular strategy. Either way, have copies of the appropriate graphic organizers available.

Eventually, students will no longer need printed graphic organizers; they will make their own to suit their learning style and the particular text they are reading. They will have integrated the reading strategies as part of the learning process in all content areas.

PART 1
Building Vocabulary

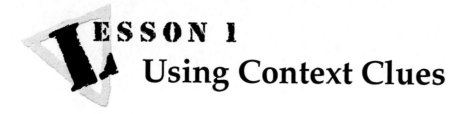

LESSON 1
Using Context Clues

Building Vocabulary

You read all the time—at school, at home, and in the community. To understand what you read, you need to understand the meanings of all of the words you come across in your reading. This section will show you some ways to build your vocabulary.

Strategies to Use

There are many ways to build vocabulary. For one, you can look up every new word. Doing this takes a lot of time, though. It also interrupts your reading. There are easier ways to figure out the meaning of a new word. You can check for context clues, recognize word parts, and look for words within words.

Analyzing Context Clues

A **context clue** is a hint about a new word's meaning found in the words around it. There are many different types of context clues.

- A definition of a word may be found in the text.

  In the American South, life centered around the **plantation,** which was <u>a large estate or farm</u>.

- A synonym (word meaning the same thing) or antonym (word meaning the opposite) may be found in the text.

  His actions were not <u>smart</u>, they were **foolish.**

- An example may help define the word.

  There are several ways to **publish** your writing, such as <u>having it printed in a book</u> or <u>posting it on the Internet</u>.

- The author may restate the word or idea.

  The man was a **migrant** worker. He would <u>move from place to place</u> to find jobs.

Context Clues in Action

The following article has examples of each type of context clue—example, definition, synonym or antonym, and restatement. See if you can guess the meanings of the underlined words from their context clues.

Using Context Clues *(continued)*

Da Vinci's Flying Machines

Leonardo da Vinci, an Italian painter and inventor, lived in the late 1400s and early 1500s. He is said to have drawn <u>prototypes</u> of the car, the submarine, the diving helmet, and the parachute. His best-known inventions, though, are his flying machines. To figure out how a flying machine might work, da Vinci spent hours <u>observing</u> and watching birds in flight. Because birds flap their wings, da Vinci's earliest machines had wings that the pilot had to flap. These machines were far too <u>weighty</u> to fly. The flapping machinery made them too heavy to get off the ground. Da Vinci later switched to wings that were <u>immobile</u>, which means "fixed in place." He created something more like a glider. In modern times, people have actually flown gliders based on da Vinci's design.

Below are some ways to use context clues to find the meaning of the underlined words.

prototypes
context clue—example

I'm not sure what the word <u>prototypes</u> means. Right after it, though, the author lists types of machines. The machines listed have only begun to be used in modern times. Since Leonardo da Vinci lived hundreds of years ago, I'd guess that a prototype might be an early example of a machine.

observing
context clue—synonym or antonym

I don't know what the word <u>observing</u> means, but right next to it is the word "watching." They are both used to show how da Vinci got his ideas from birds. I think <u>observing</u> means "watching something to learn about it."

weighty
context clue—restatement

The author says da Vinci's early machines were too <u>weighty</u> to fly. In the next sentence, the author says that they were too heavy to get off the ground. I can figure out that <u>weighty</u> must be another word for "heavy."

Using Context Clues (continued)

immobile
context clue—definition

Right after the word <u>immobile</u> come the words "which means 'fixed in place.'" This makes it clear that <u>immobile</u> means "fixed in place."

Application

Read the following article and try to figure out the meaning of the underlined words using context clues.

Is It Really a da Vinci?

Leonardo da Vinci lived almost five hundred years ago. Because so much time has passed, it is hard to prove that he came up with all the machines for which he gets credit. His drawings are the only <u>evidence</u>, which means "something that can be used as proof," we have of his inventions. Some of the machines, such as one that works like a car jack to lift heavy things, are very simple and <u>practical</u>. Some people think he was drawing machines that he saw in use. Other people think, because of <u>flaws</u>, or mistakes, in the drawings, that some of the drawings were done by da Vinci's students and not by the master himself. One of his drawings, of a bicycle, was not found until 1974. Because it looks very modern, some people think it is not <u>authentic</u> but is instead a fake.

Write the definition of each vocabulary word below. Then explain the context clue you used to figure out the meaning.

1. **evidence:** _____

   context clue: _____

2. **practical:** _____

   context clue: _____

3. **flaws:** _____

   context clue: _____

4. **authentic:** _____

   context clue: _____

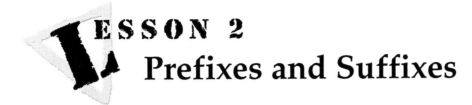

LESSON 2
Prefixes and Suffixes

Prefixes and Suffixes

Many words are made by adding onto a word that already exists. The original word is called the **root.** The groups of letters, or word parts, added to the root can change the meaning. Sometimes a new word can be broken down into a root word you know and word parts that have been added. Knowing how the word parts change the root can help you figure out the meaning of the new word.

Word parts that are added at the beginning of a word are called **prefixes.** In fact, the word *pre-* is a prefix. It means "before." The word *preschool* is made by adding *pre-* to the word *school.* Since *pre-* means "before," a preschool is a school that children go to to get ready for regular school.

Word parts that are added to the end of a word are called **suffixes.** For instance, the suffix *-ness* means "state" or "quality of." *Happiness* is "the state of being happy." Another suffix is *-ist.* It means "one who specializes in or makes." A *novelist* is "one who makes novels."

Prefixes and Suffixes in Action

Read the following article. See if you can find the meaning of the underlined words by seeing how each root word is changed by its prefix or suffix.

> ### An Accidental Success
>
> Some people follow a <u>predetermined</u> path to success. Others, like Theodore Geisel, best known as Dr. Seuss, try many things before success finds them. Theodore went to a university to become a teacher. One day, another student saw him doodling in class. She told him that he should become an <u>artist</u>. Theodore dropped out of college and became a <u>cartoonist</u>. During World War II, he made movies for the army. After the war, Theodore's publisher had an idea. He thought that Theodore's drawing style would be perfect for children's books. It was. Theodore's book *The Cat in the Hat* became an instant classic. Theodore's talent with pictures and words helped him become a success. It was his <u>willingness</u> to try new things, though, that made him one of the great children's authors of all time.

CARS: Language Arts, 5–6

Prefixes and Suffixes *(continued)*

Here is an example of how one reader used roots, prefixes, and suffixes to figure out the underlined words.

predetermined: Well, I know that the prefix *pre-* means "before." I know that someone who is determined to do something is very serious about getting it done. I also know that *determine* can be another word for *decide.* So, by putting the meanings together, I think that *predetermined* means "decided on before" or "already decided." I also think that *predetermined* has a strong meaning. Someone on a predetermined path must be very serious about following it.

artist: Well, I already know what this word means. But if I didn't, I would look first at *art.* It means "things made by painting, drawing, or sculpting." I just learned that the suffix *-ist* means "one who specializes in or makes." So *artist* means "one who makes things by painting, drawing, or sculpting."

cartoonist: I know that the word *cartoon* means "comic strip" or "funny drawing." And the suffix *-ist* means "one who specializes in or makes." *So cartoonist* must mean "one who makes comic strips or funny drawings."

willingness: The word *willing* means something like "open to trying something." I just learned that the suffix *-ness* means "state or quality." The word *willingness* must mean "the state of being open to."

Application

Here are a few common prefixes and suffixes. You will find many more as you read. Use them to help you figure out the meaning of the underlined words in the passage on the next page.

Prefixes		Suffixes	
mis-	wrong, bad	**-ist**	one who specializes in or makes
un-	the opposite of; not	**-less**	without
pre-	before	**-ness**	state, quality of being
re-	again; back	**-ful**	full of, like
		-ment	the state or act of

Prefixes and Suffixes *(continued)*

The Best Reporter in America

Nellie Bly was the pen name of Elizabeth Cochran. Born in 1864, this <u>successful</u> writer was called the "best reporter in America" by the *New York Journal.* This was at a time when most newspaper reporters were men. She was known for being <u>heedless</u> of danger. She was also one of the first reporters to do behind-the-scenes journalism. Once, she checked herself into a mental hospital for ten days. Her report on the way the hospital was <u>mismanaged</u> led to changes in the way such hospitals were run. Bly is best known for traveling around the world in 72 days. This was an <u>unheard-of</u> speed in the days before air travel.

On the lines below, write the meaning of each underlined word. Use what you know about the root word and what you can apply from your knowledge of prefixes and suffixes.

1. **successful:** _____

   _____

2. **heedless:** _____

   _____

3. **mismanaged:** _____

   _____

4. **unheard-of:** _____

   _____

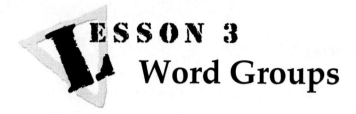

LESSON 3
Word Groups

Word Groups You have learned that adding prefixes and suffixes to words can change their meanings. Sometimes adding a suffix also changes the way a word is used in a sentence. Adding a suffix can change a word's part of speech. A verb can become a noun. A noun can become a verb. A noun or verb can become an adjective or adverb.

You can sometimes figure out what a word means if it has a familiar suffix. Remove the suffix and see if you know the meaning of the root word. Then combine the meaning of the root and the meaning of the suffix to get the meaning of the new word.

Common Suffixes One common suffix, **-ly,** is used to change nouns, verbs, and adjectives into adverbs.

Adverb Suffix	
-ly	like, in a certain way (*quietly*)

Here are some suffixes that are used to make nouns:

Noun Suffixes	
-ity	the quality of (*oddity*)
-ment	the state or act of (*amazement*)
-ness	the state or quality of being (*openness*)
-tion	the action or state of being (*prevention*)

Here are some suffixes that are used to make verbs:

Verb Suffixes	
-ate	to cause to be (*liquidate*)
-en	to become or make (*lighten*)
-ify, -ize	to cause something to be (*beautify*)

Word Groups *(continued)*

Here are some suffixes that are used to make adjectives:

Adjective Suffixes	
-able	possible to be or make (*understandable*)
-ful	full of (*thoughtful*)
-ish	like something (*babyish*)
-less	without (*bottomless*)
-ous	having a quality (*mysterious*)

Word Groups in Action

Read the following paragraph. Pay close attention to the underlined words. See if you can figure out the meaning of each word by first finding the suffix, then finding the root word.

An Amazing Victory

The Tour de France is one of the most difficult bicycle races in the world. Lance Armstrong has won this race more times than any American in history. Would you believe that, at one time, Lance had a very <u>dangerous</u> form of cancer? Doctors believed his cancer had less than a 50-50 chance of being <u>survivable</u>. Before Lance's experience with cancer, he had never even finished a Tour de France. The medicine Lance took to treat his cancer made him <u>sickly</u> and unable to eat. When Lance's treatment was over, his weight had dropped from 175 pounds to less than 160 pounds. This meant that he had a lot less weight to carry up the high mountains of the course. After taking time to train and <u>strengthen</u> his body for cycling, Lance was able to win his first Tour de France.

Here is how you might use suffixes and roots to figure out the underlined words.

The word *danger* I know very well. It means "risk of harm." The suffix *-ous* means "having a quality." Something *dangerous* must "have the quality of risking harm."

I know that the suffix *-able* means "possible to be." The second underlined word begins "surviv." The root word is probably *survive*. Since *survive* means "to live through," the word *survivable* means "possible to be lived through."

Word Groups *(continued)*

The suffix *-ly* means "like or in a certain way." I know what the word *sick* means. *Sickly* must mean "in a sick way." It describes how the medicine made Lance feel.

Finally, the suffix *-en* means "to become or make." *Strength* is a word I know well. It is another word for "power." I guess *strengthen* means "to make more powerful."

Application

Read the following paragraph. As you read, look at the underlined words and try to figure out their meanings. First, remember the meaning of the suffix. Then look for a root word that you already know. Put these two meanings together to find the meaning of each underlined word.

A Monumental Task

The faces of four <u>famous</u> presidents tower over the Black Hills of South Dakota at Mount Rushmore. This monument was the dream of Senator Peter Norbeck and artist Gutzon Borglum. It took 14 years for their dream to be <u>realized</u>. In 1927, when work began, the site was isolated. New roads had to be built. A power plant had to be built to <u>electrify</u> the site. All of this took money—<u>exactly</u> $989,992.32. In 1929, the Great Depression began. There was a <u>scarcity</u> of funds. Money ran out for the Mount Rushmore project. Still, Borglum was <u>hopeful</u> that Senator Norbeck would find new funding. <u>Amazingly</u>, Norbeck came through. In 1941, Mount Rushmore was finished.

Word Groups *(continued)*

Read the definitions that follow each word below. Circle the letter of the definition that is closest in meaning to the underlined word. Then explain how you figured out the meaning of the word.

1. famous

   (a) hungry   (c) wise
   (b) well-known   (d) good-looking

   _____

   _____

   _____

2. realized

   (a) achieved   (c) destroyed
   (b) understood   (d) begun

   _____

   _____

   _____

3. electrify

   (a) to cause to be hot   (c) to give power to
   (b) to create   (d) to bring in

   _____

   _____

   _____

4. exactly

   (a) around   (c) under
   (b) no more than, no less than   (d) in a bad way

   _____

   _____

   _____

Word Groups *(continued)*

5. scarcity

    (a) large amount   (c) weakness

    (b) sadness   (d) small amount

_____

_____

_____

6. hopeful

    (a) confident   (c) angry

    (b) patient   (d) eager

_____

_____

_____

7. amazingly

    (a) in a smart way   (c) in a slow way

    (b) in an unbelievable way   (d) in a confusing way

_____

_____

_____

PART 2
Prereading

LESSON 4
Previewing

Many people think that reading only involves looking at words on a page. Good reading, however, means doing a little bit more. When you learn the steps to good reading, you will find reading easier. You will also get more out of what you read.

The Reading Process

There are three stages to reading:
- Prereading (before reading)
- During Reading
- Postreading (after reading)

Prereading

Prereading includes four steps: Preview, Predict, Prior Knowledge, and Purpose. You can remember these steps by thinking of them as the "4 Ps."

Previewing

Previewing is taking a quick look at a reading before trying to understand the whole thing. If you have ever watched a preview for a movie or television show, you have already done previewing. A movie preview tells you what the movie is about and shows what you can expect if you go see it. Previewing your reading gives you the same sorts of information. Previewing only takes a few minutes, but it is important. Previewing gets you ready to take in new knowledge.

Here are some things you might do when you preview a reading:
- Read the title.
- Look at drawings, pictures, and captions.
- Skim the reading to see what words jump out at you.
- Read any section headings.
- Read the first and last lines of the paragraphs.

Application

Look at the article that follows. Do not read it yet! Practice your previewing skills. Read the title. Look at the drawing. Read the headings. Read the first and last sentences. Skim the article to see if any words jump out at you and give you a clue as to what the article is about.

The Nobel Prize: A Noble Idea

Nobel's Prize

Alfred Nobel couldn't have imagined what a gift he was giving the world when he wrote his will. For the last 100 years, the Nobel Prize has rewarded the people who have given the most to humanity each year. The Nobel Prize has inspired scientists, writers, and those who work for world peace.

The Creator

Alfred Nobel was born in Sweden in 1833. As a boy, Alfred was interested in poetry and science. He grew up to be a chemist and businessman, and became very rich. Among other things, he invented dynamite. Throughout his life, he continued to write poetry and plays. He also became interested in world peace.

The Will

At the end of his life, Alfred Nobel had a lot of money. However, he had no wife or children to leave it to. He decided that his money would go into a fund. Every year the fund would be used to give five prizes. Each prize would be given for the year's most important advances in the fields Nobel loved. These fields were physics, chemistry, medicine, literature, and peace. The prizes were to be given to the most deserving people, no matter what country they came from. He explained all of this in one page of his will.

The Prize

Alfred Nobel died on December 10, 1896. His will caused problems as soon as it was read. Nobel's relatives were unhappy that they were not getting the money. The Swedish government thought that giving money to foreigners would hurt Swedish science. The person in charge of the will worked hard to get it accepted by the courts. Nobel's nephew Emmanuel settled the problems with the Nobel family. Even though the king of Sweden himself asked Emmanuel to change the will, Alfred Nobel's wishes were carried out. The first Nobel prizes were awarded five years after Nobel's death, on December 10, 1901. Nobel's will continues to be a blessing to the world today.

Previewing *(continued)*

1. What does the title suggest the article might be about?

   _____

   _____

   _____

   _____

2. What headings and words jumped out at you as you skimmed the article?

   _____

   _____

   _____

   _____

3. What did the drawing suggest about the article?

   _____

   _____

   _____

   _____

4. What key words did you see in the first and last sentences that gave you a hint about the article?

   _____

   _____

   _____

   _____

LESSON 5
Predicting

Predicting

The second of the 4 Ps is **predicting.** Predicting is a part of life. Who will win when the best team in the league plays the worst team? What will happen if you sleep in on a weekday? How do you know? Using clues that come from what you see, hear, or know helps you figure out what is likely to happen in the future. Because the best team in the league has beaten better opponents in the past, it will probably beat the worst team, too. If you sleep in, you probably will not get to school on time.

Sometimes things do not happen the way you predict they will. Most of the time, though, if you look carefully at the clues, your predictions will be correct.

In reading, you use predicting the same way. You look at clues from what you read, see, or already know to figure out what information you are likely to get from the reading.

Application

When you previewed the article about the Nobel Prize, you gathered clues about it. The next step is to make predictions based on those clues. Use your predicting skills to answer the following questions about the article.

1. What does the title suggest the article is about? _____

_____

2. Who do you think the article focuses on? _____

What clues tell you that? _____

_____

3. What does the drawing suggest to you about the article? _____

_____

What clues tell you that? _____

_____

4. What do the first and last lines tell you the article might be about?

_____

_____

ESSON 6
Prior Knowledge

**Prior
Knowledge**

The third of the 4 Ps is **prior knowledge.** The word *prior* means "before." Prior knowledge is what you know about a subject before you begin a new reading about it.

Prior knowledge is everything you have learned in your whole life. Everything you have read about, seen, done, heard about, or listened to is part of your prior knowledge. Sometimes a word or a phrase triggers other ideas in your mind. This is your brain connecting the new idea to your prior knowledge. When you apply your prior knowledge before you read, your reading is more meaningful. The new information can combine with what you already know to give you a deeper understanding of the subject. When you finish a reading, the information you learn from it becomes part of your prior knowledge.

Application

Look again at the article about the Nobel Prize. You have previewed it and predicted what it will be about. Now, apply your prior knowledge to your preview and predictions.

1. One way to connect to what you already know is to brainstorm words that are related to the topic. You have predicted that the article is about the Nobel Prize. On the lines below, quickly write any words that come to your mind when you think of the word *prize*. Another word from the title is *noble*. What do these words mean to you?

prize   **noble**

_____   _____

_____   _____

_____   _____

_____   _____

Prior Knowledge *(continued)*

2. Next, write some sentences about the topic of the article. While previewing the article, you may have noticed the word *will* in the first and last sentences and in a heading. Do you know what a will is? Write what you already know about wills.

____

____

____

____

____

3. Finally, do you know anything about the Nobel Prize? Have you heard or read anything about it in the past? Do you know any people who have won the prize? If so, write what you already know.

____

____

____

____

____

LESSON 7
Purpose

The Reader's Purpose

The fourth "P" in prereading is **purpose.** A purpose is a reason for doing something. When you read, you have a purpose for reading. Here are some reasons why you might read something:

- to have fun
- to learn something new
- to find specific information

Sometimes you might read for more than one purpose. For instance, when you read the newspaper to find out what is going on in the world, you are trying to learn something new. Along the way you might gain some specific information and have fun as well.

The Writer's Purpose

Writers have a purpose for writing, too. A writer might want to entertain, to teach a lesson, or to present some specific information. Sometimes a writer will write for more than one purpose. Writers' experiences and prior knowledge also affect their writing and their purpose. Figuring out an author's purpose will help you understand what you read.

Application

Why do you think the author wrote the article about the Nobel Prize? To entertain? To teach? To present specific information? Write a sentence or two explaining what you think the author's purpose was.

_____

_____

_____

Prereading Review

Now go back and read the article about the Nobel Prize. When you have finished, think about the prereading strategies. Did the previewing, predicting, prior knowledge, and purpose steps help you understand what you read?

Purpose *(continued)*

Now look at the chart below. It is called a **4-P chart.** You can use it any time you are about to read something new. After you have practiced the prereading strategies, you will be able to picture this chart in your head. For now, use it to help you before you read.

Look at the information that you gathered in Lessons 4 through 7 about "The Nobel Prize: A Noble Idea" on page 15. Fill in the 4-P chart below, using that information.

4-P Chart

1. Preview	2. Predict	3. Prior Knowledge	4. Purpose
Words, graphics, captions, headings, subheadings that jump out	Based on Preview, what is this reading mostly about?	What do I already know about this subject? Words, phrases, figures, facts	What do I want to accomplish/ get from this reading?

PART 3
Reading Strategies

LESSON 8

Introduction to Reading Strategies

You have learned the 4 Ps, strategies to use before you read. There are also strategies to use *while* you read. In this section, you will learn about five graphic organizers that can help you get more from your reading.

Graphic Organizers

A graphic organizer is a way of showing information to make it easier to understand. You may already make graphic organizers, such as "to do" lists. There are many examples of graphic organizers in this book. You can also make graphic organizers of your own.

Writing information helps you remember it. Using a graphic organizer puts information into a form you can "see." It also puts the information into a shorter form that you can easily refer to later.

Kinds of Graphic Organizers

Graphic organizers can be changed based on what you are reading. In fact, it is very helpful to do so. Below are some useful graphic organizers.

- **KWL:** This stands for **K**—what you **know** (prereading); **W**—what you **want** to know (prereading); and **L**—what you **learned** from the reading (postreading).
- **SQ3R:** This stands for **S**—survey (prereading); **Q**—question: what is this reading about? (prereading); **R**—read: read the text; **R**—recall: recall what you have read; and **R**—reflect: think about what you have read and connect it to what you already know.
- **Semantic Web:** This graphic organizer can help you both before and after you read. *Semantic* means "related to words and their meanings." A web links things together to show how they are connected. A semantic web shows how words and ideas relate to one another.
- **Outline:** This during-reading strategy helps you list the most important parts of what you read.
- **Double-Entry Notes:** This strategy can be used both during and after reading. First, you write what is important in your reading. Then you ask yourself what you think and how you feel about the information.

KWL

KWL

The KWL chart is a graphic organizer that can help you get more from your reading. It is a great tool to use when you are reading for information. The KWL chart will help you make predictions about your reading. It will also help you apply your prior knowledge. After you have finished reading, the KWL chart will help you sum up what you have learned.

The letters of the KWL chart mean

- K—What do I **know**?
- W—What do I **want** to know?
- L—What have I **learned**?

To use the KWL chart, ask yourself the questions represented by the letters K, W, and L. Ask yourself the first two questions **before** you read.

1. What do I KNOW about this topic?
2. What do I WANT to know about this topic?

Ask yourself the last question after you finish reading. This helps you make sure you found the information you were looking for in the reading. You can also add anything else you learned as you read.

3. What have I LEARNED from my reading?

Remember, the KWL chart works best when you are reading for information. A KWL chart looks like this:

K	W	L
What I KNOW	**What I WANT to Know**	**What I LEARNED**
Use your prior knowledge to write ideas about the topic.	Write any questions about the topic that you want answered.	Write the answers to your questions and anything else you learned while you read.

Read the following short article. Then look at how a KWL chart for this article might be filled out.

Davy Crockett: Frontier Congressman

The name Davy Crockett brings to mind a brave frontiersman and soldier. Few people these days remember the time he spent in government. Even though Crockett had only six months of education, he was elected as a Tennessee state representative in 1821. He was later elected to three terms as a U.S. congressman. The pioneers in early Tennessee thought that Crockett was one of them. They thought he would fight for their views in Washington. Crockett did try to get laws passed to help small farmers on the frontier, but he did not have much success. He did not know the tricks and strategies that really got things done in Washington. In 1835, he lost his last election.

K **What I KNOW**	W **What I WANT to Know**	L **What I LEARNED**
• Davy Crockett was a famous pioneer. • Congress makes laws for the United States.	• What does Davy Crockett have to do with Congress? • Why might Davy Crockett have become a congressman? • What did he do as a congressman?	• Crockett was elected as a state representative, then as a congressman. • Settlers thought he would fight for them. • He did not get laws passed. • Crockett was from Tennessee.

Application   Here is an article called "The Game of *La Crosse.*" Below it is a blank KWL chart. Use your 4 P prereading strategies to answer the first question: What do I KNOW? Fill in this part of the chart. Next, fill in the second part of the chart: What do I WANT to know? Then read the article.

The Game of La Crosse

French settlers in the 1600s and 1700s watched Native Americans play a fast-paced game. Players used a stick with a small pouch on the end to hurl a wooden ball at a goal. The French called the game *la crosse,* or "the stick." Native Americans from the southeastern United States to the Great Lakes played *la crosse.* The game had many functions. It was played as a religious ritual and as training for war. It was also used to settle disputes between tribes. Participants, as well as those who just watched, bet money on the game. Lacrosse became an organized sport in 1856. At that time, Canadian George Beers wrote a set of rules for the game. Lacrosse has gained in popularity since then, becoming Canada's official summer sport in 1995.

Now check your questions and fill in the last part of the chart: What I LEARNED.

K What I KNOW	W What I WANT to Know	L What I LEARNED

QUIZ: "The Game of *La Crosse*"

Answer the following questions.

1. Use context clues to discover the meaning of the word *participants.* Circle the letter of the definition that is closest to it in meaning.

    (a) organizers
    (b) watchers

    (c) players
    (d) referees

    What clues did you use to get your answer? _____

    _____

2. How did this sport get the name *lacrosse?*

    (a) Lacrosse is what Native Americans called it.
    (b) The name comes from a French word.
    (c) Settlers invented the game and named it after their leader.
    (d) George Beers named it when he wrote out the rules.

3. How do you think today's lacrosse might differ from the game played by Native Americans?

    _____

    _____

    _____

4. Why do you think Native Americans might have chosen lacrosse as a way to settle disputes?

    _____

    _____

    _____

5. Why do you think lacrosse has become so popular today?

    _____

    _____

ESSON 10
SQ3R

SQ3R

The next tool to help you organize your reading is the SQ3R chart. Each letter in SQ3R stands for one of the steps to fill out the chart. SQ3R stands for

S—**survey**
Q—**question**
R (1)—**read**
R (2)—**recall**
R (3)—**reflect**

To begin filling out an SQ3R chart, use your 4 P prereading strategies. These strategies will help you **survey** your reading. Preview what you are about to read. Write anything that pops out at you. Also note anything that your prior knowledge brings to mind about the topic.

The next step is to **question.** Write any questions you think of as you survey the reading.

Then **read** the selection. Write any answers to your questions that you come across.

After reading, **recall** what you have read. Write what you remember about the reading. Make sure you understand the important facts and main ideas.

Finally, **reflect,** or think about what you have read. Write any new ideas, questions, or thoughts you have about the reading. This will help you fit the new information into your prior knowledge.

Here is what an SQ3R chart looks like.

S Survey	Q Question	R Read	R Recall	R Reflect
Preview	Ask questions	Read	Remember	Ask: What do I think?

SQ3R in Action

Look at the paragraph below. Begin using your SQ3R strategies by surveying the paragraph. Check the title. Read the first and last lines. Next, ask some questions about the reading. What do you want to know about this topic? Then read the paragraph.

The Poisonous Residents of Queensland

Queensland, Australia, is the poisonous snake capital of the world. Twenty deadly or dangerous snakes call Queensland home. The inland tiapan has the most deadly venom of any snake in the world. It is 50 times more poisonous than an Indian cobra! The eastern brown snake is slightly less poisonous, but more dangerous. Unlike the inland tiapan, the eastern brown is very aggressive. It is more likely to attack if disturbed. Despite Queensland's large number of deadly snakes, less than one person per year dies from a snakebite. These snakes use their poison to hunt. They only bite humans if they are threatened or hurt.

Now that you have finished reading, look at the SQ3R chart below. Would you have filled in the chart the same way? What do you recall as the main idea of the paragraph? What do you think about the article? What did you learn? What will you remember? What new questions do you have?

S Survey	Q Question	R Read	R Recall	R Reflect
• poisonous snake capital of the world • most deadly venom • use poison to hunt	• Why is it the poisonous snake capital of the world? • Which snakes? • How dangerous are they? • Why do snakes like Queensland?	• 20 dangerous snakes live there. • The inland tiapan and eastern brown are the only ones mentioned. • less than one death per year • not answered	• The inland tiapan has the most deadly venom of any snake. • The eastern brown is more aggressive. • Snakes only bite people if they are threatened or hurt.	• Many people are afraid of snakes even though other things hurt a lot more people. I wouldn't want to live in Queensland.

Application   Before you read the article below, use your 4 P strategies to survey it. Write your notes in the Survey column of the blank SQ3R chart below. Then write any questions in the Question column. As you read, write the answers to your questions in the Read column.

Six Flags Fly Over Texas

Since the coming of the Europeans, the flags of six nations have flown over the area now known as Texas. The first flag in Texas was planted by Spanish explorers. The Spaniards mapped the coast in 1519 and explored the wilderness, but did not start any colonies. In 1685, LaSalle, a French explorer, claimed east Texas for France. He founded Fort St. Louis, the first French colony. The colony was doomed by a series of disasters. In 1689, an expedition from Mexico found the colony abandoned. With the French gone, the Spanish regained control of Texas. They ruled it as part of Mexico and started many new colonies. When Mexico gained independence from Spain in 1821, the new nation's flag was flown in Texas. Fifteen years later, in 1836, colonists from the United States revolted against Mexico. They created the independent Republic of Texas. Texas later joined the United States for protection. It became the 28th state. When southern states broke away from the United States in 1861 to form the Confederacy, Texas broke away as well. In 1865, after the Civil War, Texas rejoined the Union. The flag of the United States has flown over Texas ever since.

Fill in the Recall and Reflect columns. What is the article's main idea? What do you think about the article?

S Survey	Q Question	R Read	R Recall	R Reflect

◤ QUIZ: "Six Flags Fly Over Texas"

Answer the following questions.

1. Use context clues to figure out what the words below mean. Then look at the definitions that follow each word. Circle the letter of the definition that is closest in meaning.

   colony
   (a) a group of people living in a new land
   (b) an army sent to take over a new place
   (c) a business built to make something new
   (d) a monument to a famous person

   abandoned
   (a) doing well
   (b) defended
   (c) rebuilt
   (d) empty

2. Which sentence below best describes the main idea of the article?
   (a) Texans have always fought to create a new government.
   (b) Many different European countries have built colonies in Texas.
   (c) The six flags represent different chapters in the history of Texas.
   (d) Texans have always struggled to be part of the United States.

Answer these questions in complete sentences.

3. What do you think could have happened to Fort St. Louis, the French colony?

   _____

   _____

4. Why do you think people might want independence from their government?

   _____

   _____

Semantic Web

Semantic Web

A third way to keep track of information is called a **semantic web.** This graphic organizer shows how ideas are related. Before you read, you can use it to brainstorm what you already know about a topic. You can use it after you read to sort information. The web will help you see how things are connected. It can also help you find the main ideas in your reading. A semantic web is useful whether you are reading for fun or reading to learn something new.

Semantic Web in Action

The reading passage below is about *The Lord of the Rings.* The semantic web that follows it shows you how someone might use a web while reading. Use your 4 P strategies to preview the article. Then read the passage. Finally, study the semantic web. Is there anything you would change?

J.R.R. Tolkien's Creation

For years, *The Lord of the Rings* has delighted readers with a magical world of elves, orcs, and mighty warriors, and the struggle of good against evil. This epic story has defined fantasy writing. It came from the mind of J.R.R. Tolkien, a professor of English. Begun in 1938 as a follow-up to his popular book *The Hobbit,* the story took 16 years to write. Some of its darkest chapters were written during World War II. Tolkien denied that the war had any effect on his writing, though. Instead, the world of *The Lord of the Rings*—Middle-earth—grew out of his love of old Viking tales. Tolkien also loved to make up his own languages. He imagined Middle-earth as the place where these languages were spoken.

Semantic Web *(continued)*

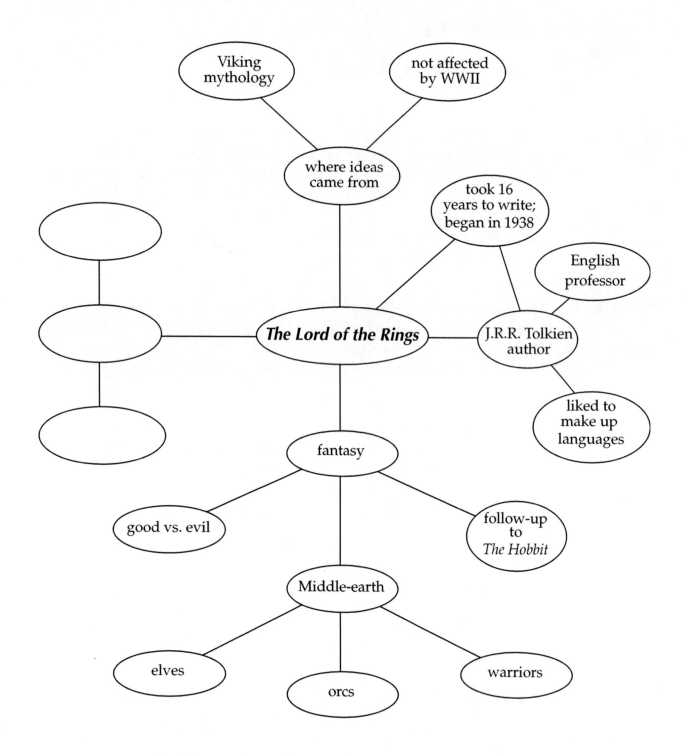

Is this semantic web organized the way you would do it? If not, change it. A graphic organizer is meant to help you get the most out of your reading. Would you add any other categories or pieces of information? Fill in anything you think is missing. Add more circles as needed.

Semantic Web *(continued)*

Application   Before you read the article below, preview it. Look at the title. Brainstorm what you know about Susan B. Anthony and women's rights. Write any ideas from your prior knowledge in the web. After you read the article, write any new facts in the other circles. Add as many circles as you need to organize your information the way you want.

Susan B. Anthony—Pioneer for Women's Rights

Imagine being an adult and not being able to vote or control your own property. This is the situation women faced in 1820 when Susan B. Anthony was born. Her parents were Quakers. Quakers were some of the first Christians to treat men and women equally. She first became part of the women's rights movement when she was working as a teacher. She learned that the men she worked with were paid five times her salary. For the rest of her life, she worked tirelessly to win the right for women to vote. She was also active in the abolitionist movement, which fought to end slavery. The Fourteenth Amendment was passed when the Civil War ended. This law gave voting rights to all citizens regardless of race. Anthony felt that, because of the new law, women should be able to vote as well. Not everyone agreed. When she voted in the 1872 presidential election, she was arrested for violating voting laws. Still, she continued to travel around the country, speaking and writing about women's rights. Until her death in 1906, she believed that voting rights for women were just around the corner. The Nineteenth Amendment, which gave women the right to vote, was not passed until 14 years later.

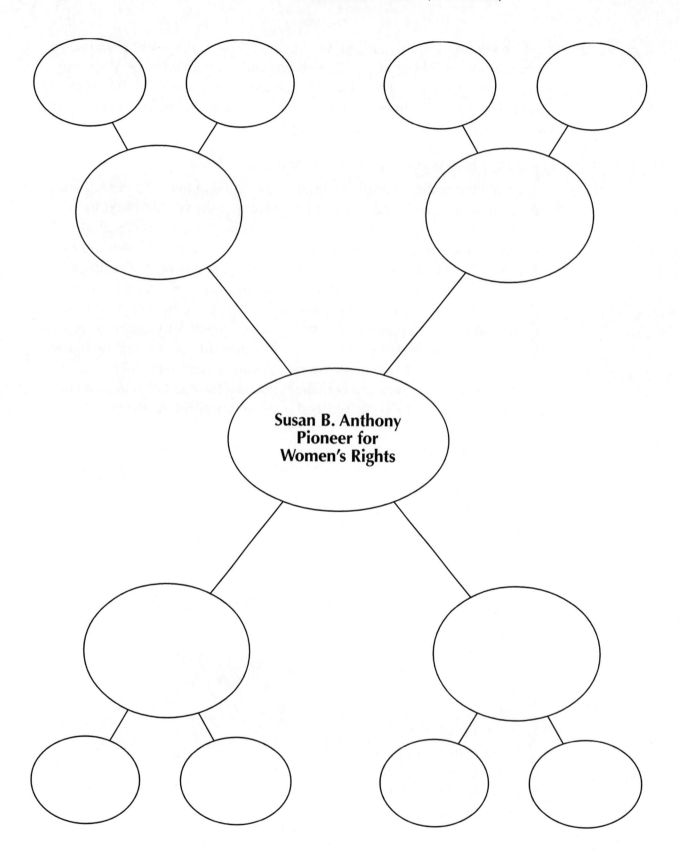

Susan B. Anthony
Pioneer for
Women's Rights

QUIZ: "Susan B. Anthony—Pioneer for Women's Rights"

1. Use context clues to figure out the meanings of the words below. Then read the definitions that follow each word. Circle the letter of the definition that is closest in meaning.

   salary
   (a) money given by the government
   (b) money paid in order to get a job
   (c) money one earns by working
   (d) money given to men and not to women

   abolitionist
   (a) a person against slavery
   (b) a person for women's rights
   (c) a person against women's rights
   (d) a person for higher teacher pay

   violating
   (a) breaking or disregarding
   (b) speaking about or expressing
   (c) trying or doing
   (d) wanting or needing

2. Why did Susan B. Anthony vote in the 1872 elections?
   (a) She believed that the Fourteenth Amendment gave her the right to do so.
   (b) When the slaves were freed, women were given equal rights as well.
   (c) She went to court to win the right to do so.
   (d) Everyone agreed that she should.

3. What are three reasons why Susan B. Anthony fought for women's rights?

   _____

   _____

   _____

4. How do you think Susan B. Anthony's early life as a Quaker affected what she would do later in life?

   _____

   _____

LESSON 12
Outline

Outline

When you were younger, did you ever color in a coloring book? A picture in a coloring book is made up of shapes surrounded by heavy outlines. The outlines define the shapes and hold the different areas of color together. In the same way, you can use an **outline** for your reading. When you create an outline for your reading, you create a structure that holds your reading together.

An outline is a great way to organize what you read. Making an outline also helps you take notes as you read. It helps you figure out the main ideas of your reading. By using an outline, you can organize the details that support each idea.

Making an Outline

Here are the steps for making an outline.

1. Create a title. This is usually the title of your reading.

2. Write a Roman numeral I. This is where you write the first main idea of the paragraph or article you are reading. Each main idea or topic that follows will be listed next to a Roman numeral. The second main idea is Roman numeral II. The third is Roman numeral III, and so on.

3. Under each Roman numeral, list the first supporting detail next to a capital letter, starting with the letter A. Each detail that supports this idea gets its own letter. Usually there will be two to four letters under each Roman numeral. Indent the letters to make your outline easier to read.

4. If more details support the ideas listed next to capital letters, you can list these details next to Arabic numbers. Start with the number 1. Indent these entries further to keep your outline easy-to-read.

Outline *(continued)*

Outline in Action

Read the following article about Ray Charles. As you read, think about the main topics of the article. Then see how an outline is created.

> ### *Ray Charles Makes It Big*
>
> The musical genius Ray Charles was born to a poor family in Albany, Georgia, on September 23, 1930. It was the beginning of the Great Depression. Times were especially tough for African Americans. By the time he was seven, Ray had completely lost his sight. Then he went to St. Augustine's school for the blind, where he learned how to read music and play the piano. He left school in 1945 to start a career in music. For years he played dances and clubs in Florida. Then he moved to Seattle, where he met Jack Lauderdale, the owner of Swingtime Records. In 1950, Ray made his first record. Ray Charles went on to become one of the greatest rhythm-and-blues musicians of all time.

Here is how you might create an outline for this paragraph.

First, look for a title. Use the title as the heading of your outline. Next, look for the main ideas in the article. To find a main idea, ask yourself, *What are the most important ideas in this article?* For this article, you might answer, *One of the main ideas is that Ray Charles had a hard time early in life.* Another idea might be, *Music turned Ray Charles' life around.* Now start your outline by writing the title and the first main idea.

Ray Charles Makes It Big

I. Ray Charles had a hard start in life.

Next, you might fill in some details under that main topic.

    A. He was born poor in 1930.

        1. It was the Great Depression.

        2. Times were hard for African Americans.

    B. He lost his sight by the time he was seven.

Next, write the second main idea.

II. Music turned Ray's life around.

Add the details.

    A. He learned to play piano at St. Augustine's school.

    B. He started a musical career in 1945.

    C. He played dances and clubs in Florida.

    D. He moved to Seattle.

        1. He met Jack Lauderdale.

        2. He made a record in 1950.

The whole outline would look like this:

Ray Charles Makes It Big

  I. Ray Charles had a hard start in life.

    A. He was born poor in 1930.

        1. It was the Great Depression.

        2. Times were hard for African Americans.

    B. He lost his sight by the time he was seven.

 II. Music turned Ray's life around.

    A. He learned to play piano at St. Augustine's school.

    B. He started a musical career in 1945.

    C. He played dances and clubs in Florida.

    D. He moved to Seattle.

        1. He met Jack Lauderdale.

        2. He made a record in 1950.

Application   Read the article "New Dinosaurs of South America." Then fill in the outline on the next page with the main ideas and supporting details that you find in the article. Add any extra lines you need.

New Dinosaurs of South America

For many years, the mighty *Tyrannosaurus rex* was thought to be the largest carnivorous, or meat-eating, dinosaur. Recent finds in South America, though, have caused the king of the dinosaurs to lose his crown. In 1993, scientists discovered the giganotosaurus in Argentina. Thought to have been 45 feet long and to have weighed 6 to 8 tons, the giganotosaurus was 3 tons heavier than *Tyrannosaurus rex*.

This titanic monster had a six-foot-long head. His eight-inch teeth were perfectly shaped for slicing through flesh. In 1997, scientists found the bones of six giganotosaurs together. They were all large enough to hunt. This discovery led scientists to believe that these dinosaurs hunted in packs. Since scientists

(continued)

Outline *(continued)*

New Dinosaurs of South America (continued)

believe that giganotosaurus had to eat at least eight tons of meat each year, it must have taken a huge feast to keep six of them fed.

The plant-eating argentinosaurus could have been such a meal. Argentinosaurus, first discovered in Argentina in 1987, is the largest land animal ever found. Only neck, leg, and rib bones of this dinosaur have been located. Judging from these huge bones, scientists estimate that argentinosaurus must have been over 100 feet long. It probably weighed a whopping 85–100 tons!

I. _____

   A. _____

   B. _____

   C. _____

I. _____

   A. _____

   B. _____

   C. _____

II. _____

   A. _____

   B. _____

   C. _____

QUIZ: "New Dinosaurs of South America"

Answer the following questions.

1. Use context clues to figure out the meaning of the words below. Then write your definition for each word.

   carnivorous _____

   titanic_____

   estimate _____

   _____

2. What are two characteristics of the giganotosaurus?
   (a) It ate meat and weighed less than *Tyrannosaurus rex.*
   (b) It was discovered in 1997 and had eight-inch teeth.
   (c) It weighed six to eight tons and had a six-foot-long head.
   (d) It ate plants and was over 100 feet long.

3. What are two characteristics of the argentinosaurus?
   (a) It is the largest carnivorous dinosaur ever found and weighed 85–100 tons.
   (b) It hunted in packs and was discovered in 1987.
   (c) It was over 100 feet long, and 6 skeletons were found together in 1997.
   (d) It is the largest land animal ever discovered, and only a few of its bones have been found.

4. What do the two new dinosaurs found in South America have in common?

   _____

   _____

5. How are the two dinosaurs different?

   _____

   _____

   _____

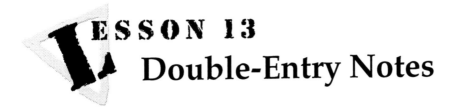

LESSON 13
Double-Entry Notes

Double-Entry Notes

Double-entry notes are another way to keep track of facts as you read. They also help you keep track of your thoughts and ideas about the reading. First, draw a line down the middle of a sheet of paper. On the left side of the chart, take notes about the main ideas of your reading. On the right side, write what you think, questions you have, or connections you make to your prior knowledge as you read.

Double-Entry Notes in Action

Read the paragraph below. Then look at the sample double-entry notes. See how you might use this strategy when you read.

The Day Baseball Was Born

The roots of baseball in the United States go deep into the country's history. Most historians agree that baseball came from rounders, an English game. Rounders was a children's game. Rules varied from place to place. In 1845, Alexander Cartwright, Jr., wrote a set of standard rules for this game. Cartwright's rules included a diamond-shaped field, the three strikes, the three outs rule, and the use of canvas bags as bases. Cartwright also started the first organized team, the Knickerbocker Base Ball Club. On June 19, 1846, the first game between two organized teams was played. The Knickerbockers played the New York Nine. This is known as "The Day Baseball Was Born."

What I Read	What I Think
• Baseball came from rounders. • Alexander Cartwright wrote the standard rules. • He started the first team. • "The day baseball was born" was June 19, 1846.	• This surprises me. I thought baseball came from another game, cricket. • Cartwright's rules sound just like the game we play today. • It's strange to think that one man started something so important in American life. • Today's games are so exciting, with the roar of the crowd. I wonder if anyone cheered for these first teams.

Double-Entry Notes *(continued)*

Application Read the article below. Then try double-entry note-taking for yourself, using the blank chart at the bottom of the page.

The Tucker

When the automobile first appeared in the United States, many independent companies sold their own brand. As time went on, companies were bought or went out of business. Eventually, most cars in the United States were made by the "Big Three": Ford, General Motors, and Chrysler. In 1946, Preston Tucker made one of the last attempts to start a large, independent car company. His car, called simply the Tucker, had many new features. These included an engine in the rear and a third headlight that pointed in the direction the car was being steered. Unfortunately, charges of fraud kept Tucker from achieving his dream. Tucker claimed that powerful car companies were trying to destroy his business. He was eventually found not guilty of the charges against him. By the time his legal problems were over, though, his money had run out. His reputation had been tarnished by the press. The Tucker Corporation was terminated. Only 51 Tuckers were ever built.

What I Read	What I Think

Double-Entry Notes *(continued)*

1. Use context clues to figure out the meaning of the words below. Then use each word properly in a sentence of your own.

    fraud _____

    _____

    tarnished _____

    _____

    terminated _____

    _____

2. Why did Preston Tucker have to stop making the Tucker?
    (a) Powerful car companies destroyed his factory.
    (b) None of his cars actually worked.
    (c) Preston Tucker ran out of money.
    (d) No one wanted a car with an engine in the back.

3. Why might a large, powerful company want to keep a small, independent company from succeeding?

    _____

    _____

    _____

4. What kind of man do you think Preston Tucker was?

    _____

    _____

    _____

5. What do you think was the author's purpose in writing this article?

    _____

    _____

    _____

PART 4
Postreading

LESSON 14
Summarizing and Paraphrasing

After Reading   Earlier, you learned how to preread by using the 4 Ps—previewing, predicting, prior knowledge, and purpose. Next, you learned five during-reading strategies to organize your reading: KWL, SQ3R, semantic web, outline, and double-entry notes.

In this section, you will be introduced to two postreading strategies: summarizing and paraphrasing. *Post* means "after." You will learn to use postreading strategies *after* you read to sum up and remember information.

Summarizing   Look at the word **summarizing.** It begins with the smaller word *sum.* In math, the word *sum* means the total of numbers that are added together. When you summarize your reading, you are also adding things together. First, you choose words or phrases from your reading that explain its main points. Then you combine these words and phrases into a new sentence or two that explain the whole reading.

Paraphrasing   Like summarizing, **paraphrasing** is a way to restate the main ideas of your reading. Unlike summarizing, paraphrasing does not use words and phrases from the reading. Instead, you restate the main ideas in your own words.

A Good Habit   Summarizing and paraphrasing are good habits to develop. These postreading strategies help you make sure you really understand the main ideas of your reading. Also, writing things helps you remember them. Postreading strategies help you remember what you have read.

You already learned to paraphrase and summarize in some of the reading strategies studied earlier. When you do the "What I LEARNED" step of the KWL chart, you are summarizing your reading. You are also summarizing when you fill in the recall part of the SQ3R chart. When you use double-entry notes, you may do some paraphrasing in the "What I Think" column. No matter which strategy you use, it is helpful to follow up your reading with summarizing or paraphrasing.

Summarizing and Paraphrasing in Action

Read the article below. As you read, look for the main ideas. Then look at the examples of a summary and a paraphrase.

Florida's Friendly Giant

If you travel the waterways of Florida, you might catch a glimpse of a large animal swimming just below the surface. Don't be frightened. This animal, the West Indian manatee, is completely harmless. West Indian manatees are found in slow-moving rivers and canals, and along the coast of Florida and Central and South America. They can be up to 10 feet long and can weigh 1,200 pounds. Like whales and dolphins, manatees are mammals. They breathe air. They have two front limbs, and their bodies taper to a paddlelike flipper. The manatee is an endangered species. Only about 3,000 manatees live in Florida. One fourth of reported manatee deaths are caused by people. For this reason, the government has taken steps to protect the manatee. Most human-related deaths occur when manatees are hit by boats. Several waterways in Florida have been set aside as manatee refuges. In these areas, boating and boat speeds are restricted so that boaters can more easily avoid manatees.

A summary puts together all the main points of the article. What are those main points?

West Indian manatees are found in Florida.
+ Manatees are mammals.
+ Manatees are an endangered species.
+ Deaths occur when manatees are hit by boats.
_____
Summary

Summarizing

Here is what a summary of the article might look like.

West Indian manatees are mammals that are found in Florida and are an endangered species, in part because they are hit by boats.

Summarizing and Paraphrasing *(continued)*

Paraphrasing   Here is an example of a paraphrase.

> The West Indian manatee, a large, harmless mammal, lives in rivers, canals, and along the coast of Florida. It is an endangered species because there are so few of them. Boating speeds are restricted in some parts of Florida because boating accidents are a major cause of human-related manatee deaths.

Application   Read the following article, using any reading strategy. Then write a summary (add up the main points and state them in a new way) and a paraphrase (restate the main ideas in your own words) of the reading.

Tales of the Roman Engineers

Tales of the ancient Romans often tell of their vast empire. An equally amazing subject, though, is their feats of engineering. The Romans built many huge structures that have survived almost two thousand years. They did this by using a material we still use today: concrete. Concrete is as strong as stone. Because it can be poured into any shape, it is much easier to work with. Concrete apartment buildings in Rome rose seven stories high.

Concrete was also used to build the aqueducts. The aqueducts are troughs, some as long as 50 miles, used to carry water into cities. They sloped from the water's source down to their destination. When the water's path led through a hill, the Romans built a tunnel. When it led through a valley, the Romans built high causeways to carry the water across. At its height, Rome had 11 aqueducts that carried water to a million people.

Summary

_____

_____

_____

_____

Paraphrase

_____

_____

_____

_____

Summarizing and Paraphrasing *(continued)*

QUIZ: "Tales of the Roman Engineers"

Answer the following questions.

1. What are two examples of Roman engineering?

   _____

   _____

2. How did the Romans build such long-lasting structures?

   _____

   _____

3. What is an aqueduct used for?

   _____

   _____

PART 5
Reading in Language Arts

LESSON 15
Common Patterns in Language Arts Reading

Do you know that you spend fourteen percent of your time reading? On the lines below, list anything you can think of that you read in a typical day.

_____

_____

_____

Did you include things like

blogs	directions	labels	recipes
calendars	e-mails	magazines	signs
captions	instant messages	maps	web pages
CD liner notes	instructions	newspaper articles	

Look carefully at what you have written and at the list above. What do many of these things have in common? Most of them are things you read to get specific information or to learn something. You probably read for fun, too. You will find, though, that you do most of your reading to get information. In school, you read to learn new things in science, social studies, math, and language arts.

As you read for information, you may notice common patterns writers use to present information. Knowing these patterns will help you identify the main ideas and details in your reading. Here are some of the most common patterns found in reading for information:

- main idea and details
- opinion supported by evidence
- compare and contrast
- cause and effect
- chronological (or sequential) order

In this section, you will learn how to identify these patterns in your reading. Recognizing these patterns will help you choose the best reading strategy for your task. This will help you gain—and retain—the most from your reading.

Main Idea and Details

Main Idea and Details

The key to reading for information is to discover the **main idea** and the **details** that support it. Every piece of writing has at least one main idea. Longer writing may have several main ideas, each with its own supporting details.

Picture a table. Imagine that the tabletop is the main idea of a piece of writing. The legs of the table are the details that support the main idea. Without the legs, the tabletop would not stand. A main idea cannot stand on its own without details to support it. On the other hand, legs without a tabletop, and details without a main idea to pull them together, serve no purpose.

To figure out the main idea of an article, ask yourself
What is (are) the main point(s) the author is trying to make?

To find the supporting details, ask yourself
What statements support the author's main idea(s)?

Application

Read the following article. Then answer the questions that follow. These questions will help you decide which statements give the main idea and which are supporting details. When you read, use any graphic organizer you like.

The Biodiesel Solution

If you have ever seen a tractor-trailer giving off a lot of smoke, you know the problem with diesel fuel. Diesel is a popular fuel for large truck engines. Diesel trucks get more miles-per-gallon than trucks that use gasoline. Unfortunately, burning diesel gives off a lot of pollution. Because so much diesel is used, diesel fumes have become a big problem.

One solution to diesel pollution is biodiesel. Biodiesel is a fuel made from vegetable oil. It can be used in a diesel engine without changing the engine much. Studies have shown that trucks that use biodiesel run as well as trucks that use diesel.

(continued)

Main Idea and Details (continued)

The Biodiesel Solution (continued)

Biodiesel is cleaner than diesel, however. Burning biodiesel releases no sulfur. Sulfur is a large part of diesel pollution. It is thought to cause acid rain. Biodiesel releases 47 percent less carbon monoxide, a chemical that is part of smog. Tests have also shown that fumes from biodiesel are about 94 percent less likely to cause cancer than diesel fumes. Biodiesel is clearly the fuel of the future.

1. Read the statements below, taken directly from the biodiesel article. In the space provided, write **MI** if the statement is a Main Idea. Write **SD** if the statement is a Supporting Detail.

   (a) Diesel is a popular fuel for large truck engines. _____

   (b) Diesel trucks get more miles-per-gallon than trucks that use gasoline. _____

   (c) Unfortunately, burning diesel gives off a lot of pollution. _____

   (d) Because so much diesel is used, diesel fumes have become a big problem. _____

   (e) One solution to diesel pollution is biodiesel. _____

   (f) It can be used in a diesel engine without changing the engine much. _____

   (g) Studies have shown that trucks that use biodiesel run as well as trucks that use diesel. _____

   (h) Biodiesel is cleaner than diesel, however. _____

   (i) Burning biodiesel releases no sulfur. Sulfur is a large part of diesel pollution. It is thought to cause acid rain. _____

   (j) Biodiesel releases 47 percent less carbon monoxide, a chemical that is part of smog. _____

Main Idea and Details *(continued)*

2. Does the main-idea-and-details organization seem like a good choice for this article? Why or why not?

_____

_____

_____

3. In what reading/writing situations would main-idea-and-details be a good pattern of organization?

_____

_____

_____

4. In what reading/writing situations would main-idea-and-details not be a good pattern of organization?

_____

_____

_____

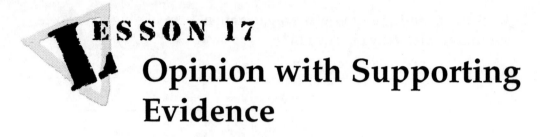

Opinion with Supporting Evidence

Opinions

Do you have strong opinions? Where do your opinions come from?

If you are like most people, your opinions are based on your tastes, likes, and dislikes. You and your friends may share some opinions. Sometimes you just like something, or you don't.

An opinion is different from a fact. A **fact** is true for everybody. It is a statement based on evidence, experience, or observation. For example, "People need air to breathe" is a fact. An **opinion** is a statement based on beliefs and feelings. For example, "I think the air in the mountains is the healthiest for people" is an opinion. If you can agree or disagree with a statement, it is probably an opinion.

When you read, you may find that some writers state their opinions as if they were facts. Be on the lookout for this. Some key words can help you figure out if a statement is a fact or an opinion.

Opinion Words		
I believe	in my opinion	perhaps
I feel	it appears	probably
I suggest	it needs to	sometimes
I think	it seems	usually

Also, look for adjectives that show someone's feelings and how that person interprets things, such as these.

Interpretive Adjectives		
brilliant	funny	mistaken
dangerous	good	safe
foolish	intelligent	ugly

Opinion with Supporting Evidence *(continued)*

Evidence
To be convincing, opinions must be backed up by evidence. This evidence must be solid facts—names, dates, numbers, or other specific information. When you read an opinion, you must look at its supporting facts. Are they strong enough to make you agree with the opinion?

Application
To see some examples of opinions with supporting evidence, look in a newspaper. On the editorial page, you will find writers who try to convince you of their opinions by backing them up with facts. The editorial page also carries letters to the editor. These come from readers who want to express their opinions.

Read the letter to the editor below. It gives one person's opinion about teaching boys and girls in separate classes. As you read the letter, look for the opinion words listed on page 58. Make up your own mind. Is the writer's evidence good enough to convince you that he or she is right? Then answer the questions that follow the letter.

Dear Editor:

In my opinion, our schools should teach boys and girls in separate classes. Every year the top-performing schools in England teach only boys or only girls. In 2001, the highest-ranked school that taught both boys and girls placed number 32 on their national exams. I believe that teaching boys and girls separately would also be good for our schools.

In classrooms where boys and girls are taught together, boys tend to hog the teacher's attention. A 1993 study showed that boys were eight times as likely to be called on in class as girls. Perhaps girls can get more of the attention they need to succeed in classes of their own. Studies have shown that, in England, girls who attend separate schools take more classes in subjects such as math and science. In schools where boys and girls are taught together, these classes are usually filled with boys.

Also, I feel that boys and girls are both more focused on their schoolwork when they are no longer distracted by each other. In 2002, the principal of Moten Elementary School in Washington, D.C., split boys and girls into separate classes. He reported that discipline problems in his school dropped 99 percent.

Opinion with Supporting Evidence *(continued)*

1. What is the author's opinion in this letter?

   _____

   _____

2. What opinion words do you find in the letter?

   _____

   _____

3. What are three facts listed in the article?

   _____

   _____

   _____

4. How do you know that these are facts?

   _____

   _____

   _____

5. Do you think the author has given good evidence to support his or her opinion? Is the opinion supported with enough facts? How do you feel about boys and girls being taught in separate classes? Why do you feel this way?

   _____

   _____

   _____

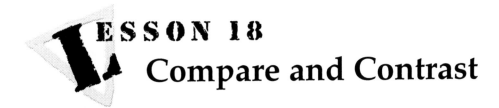

LESSON 18
Compare and Contrast

Comparing and Contrasting

Things are compared and contrasted all the time. Television ads compare and contrast different products. Politicians compare and contrast their views on important issues. What, though, does to compare and contrast really mean?

When you **compare** two things, you show how the things are **alike.** When you **contrast** two things, you show how they are **different.**

When you read for information, look for key words that show when the author is using a compare and contrast pattern. Here are some common comparing and contrasting words.

Comparing Words	Contrasting Words
also	although
as compared (to) with	as opposed to
both	but
common	contrast
further	conversely
in addition	difference
in the same way	different from
likewise	however
same as	in spite of
similar to	instead of
similarly	on the other hand
too	opposite of
	rather
	unlike
	while

Compare and Contrast *(continued)*

Application   Read the article below about two Supreme Court cases. Look for comparing and contrasting words. Then answer the questions that follow.

The U.S. Supreme Court has to balance the right to free speech with the need to keep people safe. Two cases involving students, *Tinker* v. *Des Moines Independent School District* and *Melton* v. *Young*, show how the court has worked to keep this balance.

John and Mary Beth Tinker wore black armbands to school to protest the Vietnam War. Rod Melton wore a Confederate flag patch on his jacket to show his pride in Southern history. In both cases, the school board had banned students from wearing these items to school. The Tinkers were asked to remove their armbands. When they refused, they were sent home. Similarly, Rod Melton was sent home for refusing to take off his jacket.

The Supreme Court ruled that the Tinkers had been punished unfairly. Their armbands had not disrupted classes. On the other hand, the Confederate flag had only recently stopped flying at Rod Melton's school. Fights had broken out in the town over the flag. To many people, the flag represented racism. The school board had reason to believe that Rod's patch could cause fights in school. In contrast to the Tinker case, the court ruled that Rod had been punished fairly.

1. Was compare and contrast a good way to organize this article? Why or why not?

   _____

   _____

2. What comparing words and contrasting words did you find?

   _____

   _____

3. In what reading/writing situations would the compare-and-contrast pattern work well?

   _____

   _____

4. In what reading/writing situations would compare and contrast not be a useful pattern?

   _____

   _____

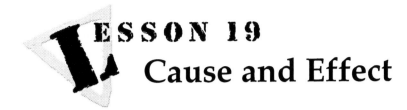

Cause and Effect

Cause-and-Effect Relationships

To explain why something happened, writers often use a pattern called **cause and effect.** For example, you know that if you stay up too late reading, you will be tired the next morning. The **cause** of your being tired is staying up too late. Being tired is the **effect** of staying up too late. You can show a cause-and-effect relationship in a chart by drawing an arrow between the cause and the effect.

Cause	→	Effect
staying up late		you feel tired

Here is how this example might read in a sentence.

Because I stayed up too late, I felt tired the next morning.

Sometimes, in your reading, you will find the effect written before the cause. For instance, *We went to the beach because it was a beautiful day.* Here the result, or effect, came first. The explanation, or cause, came second.

Effect	←	Cause
We went to the beach.		It was a beautiful day.

The key word in each sentence that shows a cause/effect relationship is *because.* Here are some other key words that will tell you when an author is using a cause/effect pattern.

as a result of	for this reason
because of	if . . . then
consequently	in order to
due to	therefore
effects of	thus

You will often find cause/effect patterns when you read for information.

Cause and Effect *(continued)*

Application Read the article below about the court case *Brown* v. *Board of Education*. Look for key words that show the cause/effect relationships in the article. Then answer the questions that follow.

One day in 1950, Oliver Brown went to enroll his daughter at the Sumner School in Topeka, Kansas. The school turned Linda Brown away because she was African-American. Therefore, Linda was told she would have to attend the Monroe School. This school for African-American children was much farther from their home. Linda's father thought this treatment was unfair, so he sued the school board. Eventually, the case of *Brown* v. *Board of Education* went all the way to the U.S. Supreme Court.

Over 50 years before, the Supreme Court had ruled in another case, *Plessy* v. *Ferguson*.

This ruling said that African Americans and European Americans could be kept separate as long as they were treated the same. Due to this ruling, many states had separate schools for the two races. These schools were anything but equal, though. Most states that had separate schools spent one quarter as much teaching an African-American student as a white student. As a result, by 1950, many African Americans refused to put up with this unfair treatment any longer. In *Brown* v. *Board of Education*, lawyer Thurgood Marshall convinced the Supreme Court to end the practice of separate schools.

1. What cause-and-effect words did you see in this article?

_____

_____

2. Was cause/effect a good pattern for this article? Why or why not?

_____

_____

3. Write the effect of this cause: Linda's father thought this treatment was unfair.

_____

_____

4. Write a cause of this effect: By 1950, African Americans refused to put up with this treatment any longer.

_____

_____

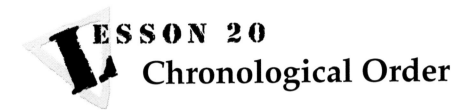

LESSON 20
Chronological Order

Chronological Order

Have you ever explained how to build or make something? Usually, the best way to do this is to give step-by-step instructions. Using words like *first*, *second*, and *next*, you explain the sequence in which things must be done.

This pattern is called **sequential** or **chronological order.** *Chronological* means "in order of time." When a story is written in chronological order, events are given in the order in which they take place. *Sequential* means "in order." Something written in sequential order presents information step-by-step to take you from start to finish.

As in the other patterns you have learned, there are key words that tell you when something is written in chronological or sequential order. Some common sequencing words are listed below.

Chronological Order Words			
after	eventually	initially	preceding
before	finally	last	since
by the time	first	later	then
continued	following	next	when
during			

Application

Read the article below about activist Cesar Chávez. Look for key words that tell you that the information is in chronological order. Then answer the questions that follow.

Cesar Chávez and the UFW

Cesar Chávez learned firsthand the bad conditions that California farm workers faced. After he finished eighth grade in 1937, he had to quit school. He went to work picking crops. Cesar spent hours doing heavy work for low pay. Eventually, Cesar decided that farm workers needed to organize. Then they could make farm owners treat them better.

In 1958, he joined the Community Service Organization. This group registered farm workers

(continued)

65

Chronological Order *(continued)*

Cesar Chávez and the UFW **(continued)**

to vote. Next, in 1962, he and his friend Dolores Huerta organized their own group. This later became the United Farm Workers (UFW). The UFW used nonviolent means, such as strikes and boycotts. They used them to make farm owners sign contracts with their workers. These contracts gave workers better working conditions and pay. One strike aimed to win contracts for grape workers around Delano, California. It began in 1965. The following year, Chávez organized a 340-mile march from Delano to Sacramento, the capital of California. This march let people around the country know about the farm workers' strike. However, it would take years of work before grape growers finally accepted their demands in 1970.

1. In what types of writing might you be likely to find chronological or sequential order?

   _____

2. Do you think chronological order was a good choice for this article? Why or why not?

   _____

   _____

3. What chronological order words did you find in this article?

   _____

   _____

4. Read the statements below. Each describes an event in Cesar Chávez's life. Without looking at the article, number the events 1–6 in chronological order. Then check the article to see if you are correct.

   __ Chávez organized a 340-mile march from Delano to Sacramento, the capital of California.

   __ Chávez and Dolores Huerta organized what would become the United Farm Workers.

   __ Chávez had to quit school to work full-time picking crops.

   __ A strike began in order to win contracts for grape workers around Delano, California.

   __ Chávez joined the Community Service Organization, which registered farm workers to vote.

   __ Grape growers finally accepted their demands.

LESSON 21
Review

You have learned some powerful reading strategies. They will help you read more effectively. In the next section, you will apply these strategies to longer readings. Before we go on, let's review what you have learned so far.

The Reading Process

Good reading is done in three stages:

1. Prereading
2. Reading
3. Postreading

Prereading

Prereading has four steps, known as the 4 Ps.

1. Previewing: scanning titles, headings, pictures, skimming for interesting words, first and last lines
2. Predicting: determining what will be in the article based on your previewing
3. Prior Knowledge: brainstorming what you already know about the topic
4. Purpose: identifying your reason for reading a given piece

Reading

Reading can be more effective when you use reading strategies and graphic organizers. You have learned about five strategies and their organizers.

1. KWL: Record *What I KNOW, What I WANT to Know, What I LEARNED* before, during, and after reading.
2. SQ3R: **S**urvey, **Q**uestion, **R**ead, **R**ecall, and **R**eflect on what you read.
3. Semantic Web: Draw a map that shows the relationships between ideas in what you read.
4. Outline: Organize topics in the reading in outline form.
5. Double-Entry Notes: Keep track of facts and your thoughts about those facts in two columns.

Review *(continued)*

Postreading

Postreading is an important step that you take after you read. It helps you check how well you understand information.

The two postreading strategies are

1. Summarizing: restating the information using words and phrases from the reading
2. Paraphrasing: restating the information in your words

Patterns of Organization

You have also learned some of the patterns writers use to present information. Recognizing the writing pattern helps you choose the best reading strategy for the job. These patterns are as follows:

1. Main Idea and Details
2. Opinion with Supporting Evidence
3. Compare and Contrast
4. Cause and Effect
5. Chronological Order

Different people read, think, and learn in different ways. You should think of the strategies you have learned as tools. When you read, select the best tool for you. You may find, as you practice these strategies, that each one works well for different types of readings. On the other hand, you may find that one graphic organizer works well for you whenever you read. Do whatever helps you to understand and to remember what you read.

PART 6
Practice
Readings

READING A

Read the selection below. Use any reading strategy you like. When you finish reading, summarize or paraphrase the reading. Then complete the quiz that follows the reading.

The Case of George Fisher

Mark Twain wrote many essays about abuses of the government of his time. This is an adaptation of his essay "The Case of George Fisher." In it he explains events that occurred after a war between the U.S. Army and a group of Native Americans called the Creek.

On the first day of September 1813, the Creek war was in progress in Florida. The crops, herds, and houses of Mr. George Fisher were destroyed, either by the Creek or by U.S. troops. By the terms of the law, if the Creek destroyed the property, there was no relief for Fisher. If the troops destroyed it, the government of the United States owed Fisher the amount involved.

George Fisher must have thought that the Creek destroyed the property. Although he lived several years after the destruction, he never made a claim on the government.

In the course of time, Fisher died, and his widow married again. Twenty years after that dimly remembered raid, the widow Fisher's new husband petitioned Congress for the damages. He backed up his claim with many peoples' testimony. This proved that the U.S. troops, not the Creek, destroyed property belonging to a peaceable citizen. But Congress did not believe that the troops were such idiots. Congress denied the petition of the heirs of George Fisher in 1832.

We hear no more from them until 1848, a full 35 years after the fields were destroyed. The Fisher heirs put in a bill for damages. The auditor who reviewed their bill gave them $8,873, half the damage suffered by Fisher. The auditor said the testimony showed that half of the destruction was done by the Creek. The government did not have to pay for that half.

That was in April 1848. In December 1848, the heirs of George Fisher pleaded for a "revision" of their bill. In order

(continued)

The Case of George Fisher (continued)

to keep up the spirits of the Fisher family, the auditor allowed them interest, or extra charges on an amount of money owed over time. They were paid interest from the date of their first petition (1832) to the date the damages were awarded. This sent the Fishers home with an additional $8,997.94. Total payment: $17,870.94.

For a whole year, the suffering Fisher family was quiet. Then they swooped down on the government once more. An official discovered one more chance for the desolate orphans. He gave them interest on the award of $8,873 from the date of the destruction of property (1813) up to 1832. Result, $10,004.89 went to the poor Fishers. Total payment: $27,875.83.

Strange as it may seem, the Fishers let Congress alone for five years. But at last, in 1854, they convinced Congress to pass a law requiring the auditor to take another look at their case. This time they stumbled upon an honest official. He said that the

Fishers were not entitled to another cent.

Another period of rest passed, until 1858. The new man in the right place was Secretary of War John B. Floyd. They came from

Florida with a rush—a great wave of Fishers. They brought the same old musty documents about the same cornfields of their ancestor. Mr. Floyd decided that the government did not owe $3,200 for trash that the Creek had destroyed, but did owe for

(continued)

The Case of George Fisher (continued)

property destroyed by the troops. This consisted of goods totaling $18,104. He allowed that sum to the starving Fishers, *along with interest from 1813.* Their ancestor's farm had now yielded to them nearly $67,000 in cash.

Does the reader suppose that was the end of it? Let the evidence show. The Fishers were quiet just two years. Then they came swarming up out of the swamps of Florida with their same old documents. They besieged Congress once more. Congress gave in on June 1, 1860. A clerk went over those papers again. This clerk found a recent forgery in the Fishers' papers. Someone had changed the price of corn in Florida in 1813 to be double the amount that had been originally claimed as the price. Nevertheless, using the forged double prices, Mr. Floyd made out a new bill. In this new bill, he laid all the damages at the door of the imbecile U.S. troops. He put everything in this time. Subtracting the $67,000 already paid to George Fisher's heirs, Mr. Floyd announced that the government still owed them $67,519.85.

Sadly enough for the poor orphans, a new president came in just at this time. Mr. Floyd went out, and the Fishers never got their money.

Adapted from Mark Twain. "The Case of George Fisher." In *Sketches Old and New* (Hartford, CT: American Pub. Co., 1875).

72

QUIZ: "The Case of George Fisher"

Answer the following questions about the reading.

1. Draw a line from each word in column A to its meaning in column B. Use context clues to figure out what the words in column A mean.

   Column A
   claim
   petition
   testimony
   desolate
   entitled
   musty
   yielded
   besieged
   forgery
   imbecile

   Column B
   smelling very old
   foolish or stupid
   qualified for or allowed
   brought in or paid
   empty or poor
   false
   request
   statements of fact
   a bill of damages
   assaulted, surrounded, or attacked

2. On what basis did the Fisher family request money from the government?

   _____

   _____

3. Do you think they deserved the money? Why or why not?

   _____

   _____

4. What kind of person do you think John B. Floyd was? How do you know?

   _____

   _____

5. How do you think the author feels about the Fishers? How do you know this?

   _____

   _____

   _____

 CARS: Language Arts, 5–6

READING B

Read the selection below. Use any reading strategy you like. When you have finished reading, summarize or paraphrase the reading. Then complete the quiz that follows the reading.

The Inspiration of Truth

In 1858, the English government declared that it would rule India. The English had been trading with India since the 1600s. By the mid-1800s, they were the most powerful force in the country. Less than 100 years later, Mohandas Gandhi and his followers forced the British to give up India. What's more, they did this, for the most part, without violence.

Gandhi had spent 20 years in South Africa. This country was also part of the British Empire. While there, he made a name for himself trying to win rights for Indian immigrants in South Africa. He had realized that Indians could show the rest of the world how unfairly they were being treated. They could do this by disobeying unfair laws, and suffering the harshest punishments, without fighting back. By showing how cruel the government was, Indians could pressure it into changing unfair laws. Gandhi called his ideas *satyagraha*, a Hindi word that

means "the power of truth." When Gandhi returned to India in 1915, he put his ideas to work at home.

During World War I, the British asked the Indians to support them. In return, the British promised to give the Indians more control of their own country. After World War I was over, nothing changed. Gandhi believed that it was time to show the British how strongly Indians felt about their freedom. He organized a *hartal*, or a day without work. All over India, shops closed and factories were empty. Some of the protests turned into riots, though. In some towns, British officials were attacked. In retaliation, British troops fired on peaceful protesters in the town of Amritsar, killing 379 Indians. Gandhi was soon arrested for turning people against British rule. At his trial, he pleaded guilty and asked for the maximum sentence. He was sentenced to six years in jail, but only served two.

(continued)

The Inspiration of Truth (continued)

In 1930, he was ready to put his ideas into action again. The British had passed a law that forced Indians to pay a high tax on salt. Gandhi and his followers set out on a 240-mile walk to the ocean. When he reached the sea, he collected some seawater in a pan. He laid the pan in the sun until all of the water had evaporated, leaving pure sea salt. He then picked up the salt and went home. From then on, people all over the country began making their own salt instead of paying the British tax. They also refused to buy other British goods.

The British soon arrested Gandhi and jailed him without trial. Protests continued, though, and in 1931, the British freed Gandhi. He went to London to talk with the British about Indian independence. Nothing came of the talks, though, and one week after Gandhi returned to India he was jailed again.

When he was released, Gandhi worked to change the Indians' way of life. He had decided that this work was more important than protesting the British. When World War II broke out, though, he was pulled back into the struggle for India's freedom. The British promised Indians self-rule after the war if they helped the British war effort. Gandhi would not support the British unless they freed India right away. The British refused, and, in 1942, Gandhi was back in jail. A wave of riots swept across India that did not stop until Gandhi went on a hunger strike. The British knew that the time had come for them to give up India. The last British governor left India in 1947.

Still, there was a defeat in the victory. When the British left India, they split it into two countries. Followers of the Hindu faith would rule India. Muslims would rule Pakistan. Violence caused by this split killed over 500,000 people and continues today. Gandhi himself was a victim of this violence. In 1948, a man who blamed Gandhi for the division of India assassinated him. Gandhi died forgiving his killer.

Gandhi's life has been an example to people all over the world. He inspired Martin Luther King, Jr., in his fight for civil rights for African Americans. Cesar Chávez used his ideas as well to win fair treatment for farm workers. Gandhi's life will continue to inspire as long as there are struggles for peace and justice.

QUIZ: "The Inspiration of Truth"

Answer the following questions about the reading.

1. Look at the definitions that follow each word below. Circle the letter of the
    definition that is closest in meaning. Use context clues to help you figure out
    the meanings.

    satyagraha
    (a) fighting for truth
    (b) sacrificing for truth
    (c) telling the truth
    (d) believing in the truth

    evaporated
    (a) poured out
    (b) dried up
    (c) became salty
    (d) was drunk

    retaliation
    (a) reward
    (b) memory of
    (c) judgment
    (d) revenge

    assassinated
    (a) given a medal for being right
    (b) insulted for an opinion
    (c) killed for a political reason
    (d) asked to speak before a crowd

2. Why did the British attack Indian protesters at Amritsar?

    _____

    _____

3. Why do you think Gandhi rejected the British offer of independence in return
    for support in World War II?

    _____

    _____

4. What pattern is the author using in this article? What key words let you know
    which pattern is being used?

    _____

    _____

5. Do you think Gandhi's methods were the right ones to use to gain
    independence for India? What would you have done if you were Gandhi?

    _____

    _____

    _____

READING C

Read the selection below. Use any reading strategy you like. After you finish reading, summarize or paraphrase the reading. Then complete the quiz that follows the reading.

From "The Life of Alexander the Great"

Alexander the Great, prince of Macedonia, conquered a huge empire. It stretched from Greece to what we now call Afghanistan. These stories were told by the Roman historian Plutarch. They show how Alexander's behavior as a youth suggested the type of man he would become.

When Alexander heard that his father Philip, king of Macedonia, had won any victory, he did not rejoice. Instead, he would tell his friends that his father would do everything. The king would leave him no chance to perform great and illustrious deeds. Alexander was more bent on action and glory than pleasure or riches. He would have preferred to become king of a land full of troubles rather than one that was flourishing and settled.

One day, a man named Philonicus brought the horse Bucephalus to Philip. Philonicus offered to sell the horse. When they went into the field, they found the horse unmanageable. He reared up when anyone tried to mount him. Bucephalus would not put up with even the voice of any of Philip's servants. They began to lead him away as untamable and useless. Alexander, who stood by, cried out. "What a magnificent horse they lose because they are not bold enough to manage him!"

Philip at first took no notice of what he said. Then Philip heard Alexander repeat this several times. He saw that his son was upset to see the horse sent away. Philip asked him, "Do you criticize those who are older than you as if you knew more and could manage him better than they?"

"I could manage this horse," replied Alexander, "better than others do."

"And if you fail," said Philip, "what will you pay for your rashness?"

"I will pay," answered Alexander, "the whole price of the horse."

As soon as the bet was settled, Alexander ran to the horse.

(continued)

From "The Life of Alexander the Great" *(continued)*

Taking hold of the bridle, he turned him toward the sun. He had noticed that Bucephalus was afraid of movement of his own shadow. Then Alexander let the horse go forward a little, still keeping the reins in his hand. He stroked Bucephalus gently when he found the horse beginning to grow eager and fiery. With one nimble leap, Alexander was atop the horse. When he found the horse free from all rebelliousness, Alexander let Bucephalus go at full speed. He sped the horse along with a commanding voice and a well-placed heel. Philip and his friends looked on in silence. They waited to see what would happen. When they saw Alexander turn the horse and return, they all burst into applause. Alexander's father, shedding tears for joy, kissed him as he came down from his horse. Philip said, "My son, seek a kingdom worthy of yourself, for Macedonia is too little for you."

After this, Philip knew that Alexander could be led to do what was right by reason, but could not be forced. He now realized that his son's education could not be trusted to ordinary teachers. He sent for Aristotle, the best-known philosopher of his time. Alexander learned a great deal from Aristotle. It is from Aristotle that he learned medicine. When any of his friends were sick, he would prescribe new foods and medicines proper to their disease. He was naturally a lover of learning and reading. He laid Homer's epic tale *The Iliad* under his pillow, claiming that it contained all military knowledge.

When Philip went away to war, he left Alexander, then 16 years old, in charge of Macedonia. Alexander was not content to remain idle. He fought against a rebellious province. He conquered its main town and renamed it Alexandropolis after himself. At a battle his father fought against the Greeks, Alexander led the charge. This early bravery made Philip proud of his son. Nothing pleased him more than to hear his people call him their general and Alexander their king.

Alexander was but 20 years old when his father was murdered. His father left him a kingdom surrounded on all sides with great dangers and fierce enemies.

Adapted from Plutarch, "The life of Alexander the Great." In *The boys' and girls' Plutarch; being part of the "Lives" of Plutarch, edited for boys and girls.* John S. White (ed.). New York: G. P. Putnam's Sons, 1883.

QUIZ: From "The Life of Alexander the Great"

Answer the following questions about the reading.

1. Draw a line from each word in column A to its meaning in column B.
   Use context clues to figure out what the words in column A mean.

   Column A
   rejoice
   illustrious
   flourishing
   untamable
   rebelliousness
   prescribe
   nimble
   rashness
   idle

   Column B
   causing great fame
   recommend
   being hasty or foolish
   doing very well
   doing nothing
   celebrate
   unable to be controlled
   lack of respect for authority
   graceful

2. How would Alexander react when his father won a victory?

   _____

3. Why was Bucephalus so hard to handle?

   _____

4. Why did Philip believe that Alexander's education could not be trusted to ordinary teachers?

   _____

   _____

5. What sort of person was Alexander? If you had known him, do you think you would have liked him? Why or why not?

   _____

   _____

   _____

READING D

Read the selection below. Use any reading strategy you like. When you finish reading, summarize or paraphrase the reading. Then complete the quiz that follows the reading.

Myths of the Vikings

The ancient Vikings lived in what we know today as Scandinavia and Iceland. Like people all over the world, the Vikings told tales of powerful gods and goddesses. These tales helped them answer essential questions, such as *Where did I come from?* and *What will happen to me when I die?* The Vikings' stories were told over and over. Through them the Vikings passed on their beliefs and values to future generations. Because we no longer believe these stories to be true, we call them *myths.*

The most important of the Vikings' gods was Odin. Odin was known as the All-Father because he slew the giant Ymir and made the world out of Ymir's body. Odin made the first man and woman out of two trees, an ash and an elm. Odin was a mighty warrior, but he also knew the value of wisdom. He sacrificed one of his eyes to gain all the knowledge in the world. He also hung from a great tree for nine days, his sword stabbing him in the side, to gain the secret of poetry. The Valkyrie, Odin's messengers, collected the bravest and most valiant warriors slain in battles and brought them to his hall, Valhalla. There, the warriors trained for Ragnarok, the great battle that would decide the fate of the world.

Frigg was Odin's wife. She was the goddess of marriage and love. It is said that she was responsible for weaving the clouds. She, like Odin, was known for her wisdom. The Vikings believed that Frigg could foresee what would happen to each god and human in the future. However, she refused to say what she knew.

Thor, the Thunder God, was the son of Odin. He was known for his great strength and his great temper. Thor's job was to protect Asgard, the home of the gods, from monsters and giants. He rode through the sky in a chariot pulled by two goats. To the Vikings, lightning was the flash

(continued)

Myths of the Vikings (continued)

of Thor's mighty hammer as he threw it across the sky. Thunder was the sound of the hammer crashing against stones, mountains, and giants' heads.

Loki was the god of mischief and cunning. Sometimes Loki got into trouble, such as the time he cut off the golden hair of Thor's wife Sif. At other times, he helped the gods by coming up with a trick or plan to solve a problem. Loki had three monstrous children. Hel was half alive and half dead. She ruled over the spirits of the dead in the cold land Niflheim. Jormungand was an enormous serpent. It was so large it could encircle the world. Fenrir was a mighty wolf. It could only be tied down by a rope made of six impossible things: a cat's footstep, a fish's breath, a woman's beard, a bear's sinews, the roots of a rock, and the spit of a bird.

Balder was a son of Odin and Frigg. He was among the best loved of the gods. One night he had a dream in which he was killed. Frigg wandered the earth making each creature, stone, and plant promise not to hurt Balder. The gods tested these promises by throwing sticks, stones, and spears at Balder. Since everything had promised to keep Balder safe, none of the stones or spears could touch him. Soon this became a sport among the gods. Loki became jealous of Balder's popularity. Disguised as an old woman, he learned from Frigg that she had not obtained a promise from one sprig of mistletoe. Loki used this sprig to make a dart. Again in disguise, he convinced the blind god Hod to hurl the dart at Balder. The dart struck Balder in the heart and killed him. As punishment for this crime, Loki was chained to a rock while a snake, which hung above him, dripped poison into his eyes.

The Vikings believed that one day Loki would escape from his chains. He would gather his children and all of the monsters and giants of the world to attack Asgard. This great battle, called Ragnarok, would be the end of the gods. Thor and Jormungand would slay each other. The great wolf Fenrir would kill Odin and swallow the sun. Great fires would burst forth and incinerate the earth, destroying everything. A few gods would survive, however, and some would come back from the dead. Two people who had hidden themselves away would come out after the battle, and the human race would be reborn.

QUIZ: "Myths of the Vikings"

Answer the following questions about the reading.

1. Look at the definitions that follow each word below. Circle the letter of the definition that is closest to the word in meaning. Use context clues to figure out the meanings.

myth
(a) a story everyone believes
(b) a story no one ever believed
(c) a story that is no longer believed
(d) a true story

encircle
(a) to swallow
(b) to wrap around
(c) to twist
(d) to outweigh

essential
(a) very important
(b) complicated
(c) easily answered
(d) silly

foresee
(a) to look through
(b) to predict
(c) to decide
(d) to stop

incinerate
(a) to cover
(b) to dazzle
(c) to clean
(d) to burn

valiant
(a) dangerous
(b) healthy
(c) weak
(d) courageous

2. What lessons could one learn from the myth of Balder?

_____

_____

3. Now that you know some of their stories, what kind of people do you think the Vikings were? What did they feel was important?

_____

_____

4. Why do you think the Vikings created a story about the end of the world?

_____

_____

5. How were the Vikings like people today? How were they different?

_____

_____

Blank
Graphic
Organizers

4-P Chart

1. Preview	2. Predict	3. Prior Knowledge	4. Purpose

KWL Chart

K	W	L
What I KNOW	**What I WANT to Know**	**What I LEARNED**

SQ3R Chart

S Survey	Q Question	R Read	R Recall	R Reflect

Semantic Web

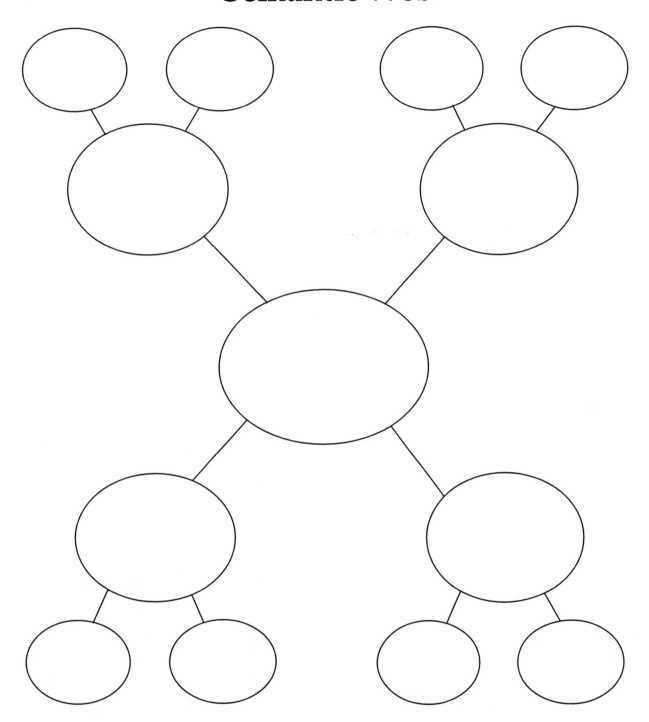

Outline

I. _____

    A. _____

        1. _____

        2. _____

        3. _____

    B. _____

        1. _____

        2. _____

        3. _____

II. _____

    A. _____

    B. _____

    C. _____

Double-Entry Notes

What I Read	What I Think

Teacher's Guide
and
Answer Key

Part 1: Building Vocabulary

Lesson 1: Using Context Clues

Application

1. **evidence:** an item that can be used as proof; context clue: definition

2. **practical:** useful; context clue: example

3. **flaws:** mistakes or errors; context clue: restatement

4. **authentic:** real or genuine; context clue: antonym

Lesson 2: Prefixes and Suffixes

You may want to remind students of a few elementary spelling rules. Point out that prefixes do not change the spelling of the word they modify, but suffixes may. When a word ends in *e*, the final *e* must be dropped before adding a suffix that begins with a vowel. For instance, *tame* becomes *tamable*. If a word ends in *y*, remind students to change the *y* to an *i* before adding the suffix, as in *merry + ly = merrily*.

Application

1. **successful:** success (accomplishment, doing well) + full of = full of accomplishment

2. **heedless:** heed (pay attention) + without = without paying attention

3. **mismanaged:** bad + managed (run) = run badly

4. **unheard-of:** heard of (known) + not = not known or never before known

Lesson 3: Word Groups

Application

1. (b) *fame + ous*
2. (a) *real + ize*
3. (c) *electric + ify*
4. (b) *exact + ly*
5. (d) *scarce + ity*
6. (a) *hope + ful*
7. (b) *amazing + ly*

Part 2: Prereading

Lesson 4: Previewing

Application

Encourage students to answer these questions aloud. Think along with them or model the answers for them.

Sample answers:

1. The title tells me that the article is about the Nobel Prize. The words "a Noble Idea" make me think the article will be about something good.

2. When I skimmed the article, I came across the name Alfred Nobel. Since his name is the same as the prize's name, maybe he started the prize.

3. The caption says "Nobel's Prize." The picture shows a circle with a person's face on it. I'll bet this is a medal awarded to the prizewinners. I wonder if that's a picture of Alfred Nobel.

4. The first sentence says that Alfred Nobel gave a gift to the world. The last sentence says Nobel's will continues to be a blessing to the world today.

Lesson 5: Predicting

Application

This activity asks students to take their preview a step further by making predictions based on the information they gathered. You may want to ask them to write one sentence that gives their prediction about the article. Then you can have them check back after they read to see if their predictions were correct.

Sample answers:

1. The title makes it clear that the article is about the Nobel Prize. Also, the subtitle "A Noble Idea" makes me think that the article will be about how the idea for the prize came about.

2. Alfred Nobel's name jumps out at me. Since his last name is the same as the name of the prize, I know there will be information about him in the article.

3. The drawing of the prize makes me certain that the article will give information about the prize. Since the caption says "Nobel's Prize," I think the article will be mostly about Nobel.

4. The first sentence talks about Nobel giving a gift to the world. This tells me that Alfred Nobel probably created the prize. The last sentence mentions Nobel's will. This gives me a clue that Alfred Nobel's will has something important to do with the prize.

Lesson 6: Prior Knowledge

Application

Encourage students to dig as deeply as they can into their prior knowledge. This step can lead to all sorts of connections and ideas. Remind students that there are no wrong answers when brainstorming. Some students may already know about the Nobel Prize. Invite these students to share their knowledge with the class.

1. Words associated with *prize* might include *reward, trophy, success, first-place, achievement, winner.* Words associated with *noble* might include *good, important, honest, honor, leader, just.*

2. Some sentences related to the topic of wills may make reference to death, inheritance, or instructions on what to do with a person's possessions when he or she dies. Encourage students to brainstorm widely on this topic. If students are stuck, ask them to think of movies, television shows, or stories that include an inheritance. Mysteries often use wills as a plot device.

3. Answers will vary.

Lesson 7: Purpose

Application

Answers will vary.

Part 3: Reading Strategies

Lesson 8: Introduction to Reading Strategies

This lesson introduces the reading strategies featured in this book. Some of these strategies may be familiar to students; others may be new.

Lesson 9: KWL

KWL in Action

You may want to model the KWL process when you introduce it to students. Help them ask themselves the correct questions.

K: To preview the article, I'm looking at the title and glancing at the paragraph to see what words jump out at me. The name Davy Crockett is a famous one. I know he was a famous pioneer. There have been many songs, movies, and books about him. I also know that Congress makes laws for the United States. The title makes it clear that Davy Crockett was a congressman.

W: The picture the name Davy Crockett brings to mind is of a hunter and woodsman. It doesn't make me think of Congress or government. I wonder how Crockett got to be a congressman? I wonder what sort of congressman he was? I wonder if he did a good job?

L: Well, I found out how Davy got to Congress and why people elected him. I also learned that he wasn't very good at his job. I also got some information that I didn't know—that Davy Crockett was from Tennessee.

Application

The KWL chart might include the following:

K	W	L
• Lacrosse is a sport that is played by tossing a ball into a net using a stick with a pouch on the end. • *La crosse* looks like it could be a French word. • Lacrosse is a popular sport in America. • Native Americans lived in North America before the Europeans came.	• *La crosse* isn't how the name of the game is spelled today. Will the article tell where the name *lacrosse* came from? • What does lacrosse have to do with Native Americans? • How are the French involved with lacrosse?	• Lacrosse was played by Native Americans for a number of reasons. • French settlers first saw Native Americans play lacrosse. • The name *lacrosse* came from the French word for *stick*.

Quiz

1. (c) players

   The context clue is an antonym. *Participants* are contrasted with *those who watched.*

2. (b) The name comes from a French word.

   This answer is stated in the text.

3. Answers will vary. Sample answer: The Native American game varied from place to place, and today's game has official rules.

4. Answers will vary. Sample answer: Playing a game like lacrosse is a safer way to settle disputes than fighting.

5. Answers will vary. Sample answer: It is fast-paced and exciting.

Lesson 10: SQ3R

Application

Sample answers:

S:

Spain, France, Mexico

Civil War

Texas

explorer, revolt, colony

1519, 1685, 1689, 1821, 1836, 1861, 1865

Six flags theme park

Q:

What are the six flags?

What happened during the Civil War?

Since these words make me think of history, how do they fit in?

Why are these dates important?

Does this have anything to do with the Six Flags amusement park?

R(1):

Spain, France, Mexico, Republic of Texas, United States, Confederacy

Texas joined the Confederacy.

Six flags = different periods in Texas history

Texas government changed on these dates.

Not answered

R(2):

Many different governments have been in charge of Texas.

There were many different reasons for these changes, including colonizations, disasters, revolutions, and people simply deciding whom they wanted to rule them.

R(3):

Texas has an interesting history. The land has changed hands many times. I'll bet other parts of the United States have changed hands many times as well.

People seem to have a strong desire to rule themselves. First, Mexico won independence from Spain, then Texas became independent from Mexico. However, the people of Texas chose to be part of the United States.

There were people in Texas before the Europeans came, but the article doesn't mention them. I wonder who they were?

Quiz

1. **colony:** (a) a group of people living in a new land

    abandoned: (d) empty

2. (c) The six flags represent different chapters in the history of Texas.

3. Answers will vary. Sample answer: They were victims of disease, bad weather, lack of food, and so forth.

4. Answers will vary. Students will answer this question based on their knowledge of history and their own feelings. Encourage students to use their prior knowledge when answering this question.

Lesson 11: Semantic Web

Semantic Web in Action

Encourage students to brainstorm what they know about *The Lord of the Rings.* Due to the popular movies, they may know quite a lot. Invite students who know about this story to explain what they know.

Application

This is a good activity to do along with your students. Invite them to share what they already know about women's rights. Then have them list everything they learned in the article about Susan B. Anthony. You can show them different ways they can organize their webs. One way might be to use the different causes Anthony supported as subtopics to which students can connect details from her life and their prior knowledge. Another might be to use the events in her life as subtopics to show how they connect to her ideals and goals. Encourage students to add as many extra circles as they need and to organize their webs in a way that makes sense to them.

Here are some facts they might include in their webs:

*   unable to vote
*   Quaker
*   abolitionist
*   teacher
*   paid one fifth of a man's salary
*   voted in 1872 presidential election
*   arrested for violating voting laws
*   Fourteenth Amendment gave all citizens right to vote
*   died in 1906
*   born in 1820
*   Nineteenth Amendment gave women right to vote

Quiz

1. **salary:** (c) money one earns by working

    abolitionist: (a) a person against slavery

    violating: (a) breaking or disregarding

2. (a) She believed that the Fourteenth Amendment gave her the right to do so.

3. Three reasons from the article are women couldn't vote; women could not control their own property; women were paid less than men for the same work. Students may think of others.

4. Sample answer: Early in life, Anthony was exposed to a society that treated the sexes equally. The shock of discovering how women were treated elsewhere in society probably had something to do with her activism.

Lesson 12: Outline

Application

Outlines may vary in their specific details or wording. Encourage students to ask themselves *What is the main idea?* and *What are the details that describe the main idea?*

New Dinosaurs of South America (title)

I. Largest carnivorous dinosaur found (main idea)

    A. Giganotosaurus found in Argentina in 1993 (supporting detail)

    B. 45 feet long, 6–8 tons (supporting detail)

    C. 3 tons heavier than *T rex* (supporting detail)

II. Giganotosaurus was a mighty predator (main idea)

    A. six-foot head, eight-inch teeth (supporting detail)

    B. hunted in packs (supporting detail)

        1. 6 discovered together in 1997 (detail)

        2. all old enough to hunt (detail)

    C. ate 8 tons of meat per year

III. Largest land animal ever found

    A. Argentinosaurus discovered in 1987

        1. only a few bones found

        2. scientists estimate size from bones

    B. 100 feet long, 85– 100 tons

Quiz

1. **carnivorous:** meat-eating

   titanic: enormous or huge

   estimate: to make a scientific or an educated guess based on evidence

2. (c) It weighed six to eight tons and had a six-foot-long head.

3. (d) It is the largest land animal ever discovered, and only a few of its bones have been found.

4. Both argentinosaurus and giganotosaurus are the largest of their kind ever discovered.

5. Giganotosaurus ate meat while argentinosaurus ate only plants. Argentinosaurus was vastly bigger than giganotosaurus.

Lesson 13: Double-Entry Notes

Encourage students to take advantage of the What I Think section to think deeply about what they read. Remind students that their ideas and opinions about their reading are as important as the information they take away from it.

Application

Here is an example of double-entry note-taking for the article on the Tucker.

What I Read	What I Think
• Independent car companies gave way to the "Big Three." • Tucker wanted to create an independent car company. • The Tucker had many new features. • Tucker was accused of fraud. • He thought enemies were out to get him. • Tucker was found not guilty. • Tucker ran out of money and had to close his company.	• I've heard of the "Big Three" car companies, but I've never heard of Tucker. • The directional headlight sounds like a cool feature. • Many people who get into trouble blame others for their problems. Still, I can see why a company might want to get rid of a competitor. • It's too bad Tucker had so many problems since he was cleared of the charges. • I wonder what happened to those 51 Tuckers.

Quiz

1. Sentences will vary. Make sure that students use the words properly. Sample answers:

   fraud: The men were accused of fraud because they were selling land that they did not own.

   tarnished: Even though he did not steal the girl's lunch, no one will trust him because his reputation is tarnished.

   terminated: The school board terminated the program due to lack of funding.

2. (c) Preston Tucker ran out of money.

3. Answers will vary. Sample answers: A large company might not want to face competition, especially if the independent company has new and innovative ideas.

4. Answers will vary. Sample answers: an independent person; someone who was not afraid to try something new; a bad businessman and a failure.

5. Answers will vary. Sample answers: to inform people about a rare automobile or an American entrepreneur; to teach a lesson about what can happen to new businesses; to entertain car fans.

Part 4: Postreading

Lesson 14: Summarizing and Paraphrasing

Application

Summary (sample answer)

The Romans built many huge structures that have survived for 2,000 years by using concrete. With concrete, the Romans built apartment buildings seven stories high and the famous aqueducts.

Paraphrase (sample answer)

Using concrete, the Romans built many structures that still survive today. They built tall apartment buildings, as well as aqueducts that carried water to their cities.

Quiz

1. apartments, aqueducts
2. The Romans used concrete.
3. An aqueduct is a trough that is used to carry water to cities.

Part 5: Reading in Language Arts

Lesson 15: Common Patterns in Language Arts Reading

Students will probably list textbooks, magazines, fiction books, and e-mails among their reading. Encourage them to stretch their idea of what reading is through brainstorming.

Lesson 16: Main Idea and Details

Remind students that being able to recognize main ideas and supporting details is crucial to understanding what they read when they are reading for information.

Application

Answers to **MI** and **SD**:

1. (a) SD   (f) SD
   (b) SD   (g) SD
   (c) SD   (h) MI
   (d) MI   (i) SD
   (e) MI   (j) SD

2. Answers will vary.

3. Answers will vary. Sample answer: when you have a statement that requires several details to fully explain or prove it

4. Answers will vary. Sample answer: writing with few details or writing that includes a lot of equally important events, such as a history or biography

Lesson 17: Opinion with Supporting Evidence

Invite students to look at examples of opinion with supporting evidence in their own newspapers. Encourage them to look for opinion words not only in what they read but also in what they hear on television, on the radio, and in conversations.

Application

Answers will vary. Sample answers:

1. The author feels that boys and girls should be taught in separate classes.

2. in my opinion, I believe, good, perhaps, I feel

3. Facts include: The top-performing schools in England teach only boys or girls; co-ed schools place much lower; boys are eight times as likely to be called on in class as girls; a principal in Washington, D.C., reported a 99 percent drop in discipline problems when boys and girls were taught separately.

4. Answers will vary. Sample answer: Actual numbers from scientific research are quoted. Data from the English national exams for a specific year are used. A principal from a specific school in Washington, D.C., is given as a source of information.

5. Answers will vary. Make sure to point out to students that the source of the "1993 study" is not given. Also note that the numbers quoted by the principal could be the result of anecdotal evidence, not of statistical evidence.

Lesson 18: Compare and Contrast

Application

1. Answers will vary. Sample answer: Yes, it showed why the two cases had different results.

2. both, similarly, on the other hand, in contrast to

3. Answers will vary. Sample answer: advertisements, political speeches, position papers, personal writing for the purpose of making a decision

4. Answers will vary. Sample answer: informational writing meant to explain one specific thing

Lesson 19: Cause and Effect

Application

1. therefore, because, so, due to, as a result

2. Answers will vary. Sample answer: Yes, it really gave the background to understand the court case.

3. Effect: He sued the school board.

4. Cause: Most states spent one quarter as much teaching an African-American student as a white student.

Lesson 20: Chronological Order

Application

1. Answers will vary. Sample answers: biographies, historical accounts, diaries, how-to books

2. Answers will vary. Sample answer: Yes, it showed how he developed into a labor leader.

3. after, eventually, next, began, following, finally

4. Correct order: 3, 5, 2, 4, 1, 6

Part 6: Practice Readings

Reading A: *The Case of George Fisher*

The outline is a good strategy for this chronologically ordered story. An outline will help students keep track of the events in the Fisher saga and the details surrounding each event.

Quiz

1. Make sure that students understand vocabulary that is crucial to understanding the story, such as *petition, claim,* and *forgery.*

   claim—a bill of damages

   petition—request

   testimony—statements of fact

   desolate—empty or poor

   entitled—qualified for or allowed

   musty—smelling very old

   yielded—brought in or paid

   besieged—assaulted, surrounded, or attacked

   forgery—false

   imbecile—foolish or stupid

2. Answers will vary. Sample answer: Their ancestor, George Fisher, had a farm that was destroyed during a battle between the Creek and the U. S. army.

3. Answers will vary. Sample answers: According to the story, the Fishers did not deserve the money. They took advantage of corrupt officials to get a greater and greater payout for the same damages.

4. Answers will vary. Sample answers: John B. Floyd was dishonest because he gave the Fishers money based on a forgery; Mr. Floyd was foolish because he awarded the Fishers additional money on claims that had already been paid.

5. Answers will vary. Sample answer: Twain does not have much respect for the Fishers. He uses ironic language, calling them desolate and starving, while at the same time describing large sums of money they are extracting from the government. Twain also

implies their dishonesty by mentioning that honest officials tend to reject their claims.

Reading B: *The Inspiration of Truth*

This reading lends itself to a variety of strategies. It is organized chronologically, and an outline would certainly be appropriate. Double-entry notes are an excellent strategy for this reading. Students can list what they learn about Gandhi and also keep track of their feelings about the things Gandhi did. Gandhi was a controversial figure during his life and was not admired by everyone. Also, KWL and SQ3R charts can help students brainstorm what they already know about Gandhi.

Quiz

1. *satyagraha:* (b) sacrificing for truth

   retaliation: (d) revenge

   evaporated: (b) dried up

   assassinated: (c) killed for a political reason

2. Answers will vary. Sample answer: The British were seeking revenge for riots and attacks on British officials during the *hartal.*

3. Answers will vary. Sample answer: The British had made the same promise during World War I and had not lived up to it.

4. Chronological order. Sequencing words include *after, during, when, finally.*

5. Answers will vary. Students will have to draw on their own beliefs to answer this question. Encourage students to discuss what they feel is the best way to solve difficult problems.

Reading C: *From "The Life of Alexander the Great"*

This selection is a good one for practicing SQ3R and KWL charts. Invite students who know about Alexander the Great to share their knowledge with the class. Double-entry note-taking also works well for these stories. Students can write what they learn on one side of the chart and their personal opinions of Alexander on the other side.

Quiz

1. rejoice—celebrate

   illustrious—causing great fame

   flourishing—doing very well

   untamable—unable to be controlled

   rebelliousness—lack of respect for authority

   prescribe—recommend

   nimble—graceful

   rashness—being hasty or foolish

   idle—doing nothing

2. Answers will vary. Sample answer: Alexander was not entirely pleased when his father won a victory because he thought that everything his father did took away from his possible future accomplishments.

3. Bucephalus was afraid of his own shadow.

4. Answers will vary. Sample answer: Alexander was headstrong; he could be convinced to do something but he couldn't be forced to do it. His teacher would have to be good enough to convince Alexander that the things he was learning were important.

5. Answers will vary. Encourage students to imagine Alexander in terms of their own lives. You can ask them such questions as *Do you know anyone who reminds you of Alexander? If Alexander were alive today, what sorts of things would he like? What do you think his favorite classes would be? What sports do you think he would play?*

Reading D: *Myths of the Vikings*

Tales of the Viking gods are fairly well-known, and references to them pop up all the time in popular culture, including the days of the week. As a result, an SQ3R chart will help students brainstorm what they already know about these stories. A semantic web is also great for this selection. The web can help students keep track of the various gods and goddesses, their attributes, and the relationships between them.

Quiz

1. **myth:** (c) a story that is no longer believed

   essential: (a) very important

   incinerate: (d) to burn

   encircle: (b) to wrap around

   foresee: (b) to predict

   valiant: (d) courageous

2. Answers will vary. Sample answer: Jealousy is a very dangerous emotion.

3. Answers will vary. Sample answer: The Vikings valued strength and courage in battle, but they also valued wisdom and poetry.

4. Answers will vary. Sample answer: Everything that has a beginning has to have an end as well. Some students may argue that the Viking story of Ragnarok is not the end of the world since some people survive and the world is reborn.

5. Answers will vary. Encourage students to think about the important questions that people are trying to answer today and the methods they use to answer them. Students can then contrast this with the way the Vikings answered their important questions.

Share Your Bright Ideas with Us!

We want to hear from you! Your valuable comments and suggestions will help us meet your current and future classroom needs.

Your name_____Date_____

School name_____

School address_____

City _____State _____Zip_____Phone number (_____)_____

Grade level taught_____Subject area(s) taught_____Average class size_____

Where did you purchase this publication?_____

Was your salesperson knowledgeable about this product?   Yes_____   No_____

What monies were used to purchase this product?

____School supplemental budget   ____Federal/state funding   ____Personal

Please "grade" this Walch publication according to the following criteria:

Quality of service you received when purchasing ....A   B   C   D   F
Ease of use...A   B   C   D   F
Quality of content..A   B   C   D   F
Page layout ....A   B   C   D   F
Organization of material ....A   B   C   D   F
Suitability for grade level ....A   B   C   D   F
Instructional value...A   B   C   D   F

COMMENTS:_____

_____

What specific supplemental materials would help you meet your current—or future—instructional needs?

_____

Have you used other Walch publications? If so, which ones?_____

May we use your comments in upcoming communications?   ____Yes   ____No

Please **FAX** this completed form to **207-772-3105**, or mail it to:

Product Development, J. Weston Walch, Publisher, P. O. Box 658, Portland, ME 04104-0658

We will send you a **FREE GIFT** as our way of thanking you for your feedback. **THANK YOU!**